~ *Vermont* ~
FARM WOMEN

❧ *Vermont* ❧
FARM WOMEN

Written and Photographed by

PETER MILLER

WATERBURY, VERMONT
www.silverprintpress.com

DEDICATION

Ignored by the government, belittled by agribusiness, considered poor risks by banks, those who own and operate small farms survive on hard work, their attachment to the earth, and their cherished independence. This book is dedicated to those women and men.

This book has been generously supported by:

CABOT CREAMERY

THE FREEMAN FOUNDATION

THE VERMONT ARTS COUNCIL

"Peace of Wild Things," page 20, from *The Selected Poems of Wendell Berry* by Wendell Berry. Copyright © 1998 by Wendell Berry. Reprinted by permission of Counterpoint Press, a member of Perseus Books, L.L.C.

Song on page 95, by Blanche Jarvis, reprinted with permission of Sylvia Jarvis

Book design by Peter Holm, Sterling Hill Productions

Published by Silver Print Press
20 Crossroad
Waterbury, Vermont 05676
E-mail: peter@silverprintpress.com
Website: www.silverprintpress.com

Printed in Canada by Friesens

First Edition: October 2002

Other books by Peter Miller:
Vermont People
People of the Great Plains
The First Time I Saw Paris
The 30,000 Mile Ski Race
Peter Miller's Ski Almanac
The Photographer's Almanac (coauthor)

Publisher's Cataloging-in-Publication Data

Author: Miller, Peter
Title: Vermont Farm Women
Published: Waterbury, VT; Silver Print Press, 2002
Documentary photos and text on Vermont farm women.
1. Vermont—Description—1998–2002
Subject:
1. Women farmers—Vermont
2. Women in agriculture—Vermont
3. Women—Vermont
4. Farms—Vermont
Material: 144 p. ill.; 24 x 31 cm.
Library of Congress Control Number: 2002093180
ISBN: 0-9628064-7-1

V 305.43 Library Cataloging Number

ACKNOWLEDGMENTS

Every book is a collaboration and so it is with my books — I seek the expertise and professionalism of the best.

The elegance of this book, and some of my other books, is due to the creativity of Peter Holm of Sterling Hill Productions. Peter is the book's designer, but he also gave advice (sometimes imperiously) on the editorial direction and helped select the photographs. He created the layouts and worked closely with the printer to assure the highest quality. Without him, the book would suffer greatly.

Jamie Gage did the initial edit. He put my fast-paced flow of words into some sort of grammatical sense. Janet Jesso's tight copy edit was wonderful. Other people who gave advice on the direction of the book and on the selection of the cover were Roberta MacDonald, Chris and Carrie Morrow, Barbara Morrow, Cameron Chalmers, and my two daughters, Hilary and Dodie. Fletcher Manley, an old friend and an ace with digital printing, finished off the scans from which this book is produced and then made the prints for the Vermont Farm Women Photography Exhibition. He is another one of those perfectionists.

I published this book myself, as I did with the other books in this series, *Vermont People* and *People of the Great Plains*. Usually, I finance the printing of the books with a bank loan, secured with my house, and it is never enough. This time I had financial help, and I might not have to max out my credit cards. Harvey and Suzy Edwards, old friends, gave me a loan when I was pretty well down and ready to give up. Susan Ritz donated money to help with the printing. I didn't know it when I first met her, but her mother and I were friends when I was twelve years old. Mary Miller, my sister-in-law and former aide to Senator Patrick Leahy, helped with fund raising. Stephanie McConaughy opened doors for me at Shelburne Farms, where a farm women photo exhibition introduced the book to Vermont. Then Stephanie used more connections to help fund raise for the exhibition. She would rather be skiing, and so would I.

But above all, I wish to thank the women who graciously gave their time so I could photograph and interview them. And I also would like to acknowledge so many other farm women who are dedicated to small farming and should be in the book. I just didn't have the time to meet you all.

CONTENTS

Foreword

The Lepine Farm on Mud City Loop road in Morristown was bought by Imelda and Maurice Lepine in 1942. Gert Lepine gave up teaching in 1952 to farm with her father, mother, and brother Lawrence. In 1963, Jeannette Lepine left her job as an airline stewardess for PanAmerican and returned to help her sister. In 1976 Lawrence left the farm. Therese, another sister, retired from working in Washington, D.C., with Senator Aiken and returned to Vermont, and thus was formed the trio of farming sisters.

The Lepine herd was one of the top-ten herds in the nation for its size. In 1996 Gert auctioned off the herd of 125 Jerseys, and buyers were calling in bids from around the nation. Her farmland of 667 acres was valued for development at $399,000. She sold the development rights to the Vermont Land Trust and Vermont Housing and Conservation Agency for $150,000. She and her sisters Therese and Jeannette still live there and are recognized as the first family of Vermont women farmers.

Life has been easier since I and my sisters retired and sold our Jersey herd. We now find time to paddle our small kayaks into ponds and drop a line. Fishing is so relaxing. We visit flea markets and attend more auctions, and I love to drive the back roads that I have never been on before. What's just over the hill? But most of all, we have time to visit, and many people drop in to chat about Vermont and farming. What I hear is encouraging and invigorating.

I have just finished reading *Vermont Farm Women*. I find it fascinating reading, for it features women farmers from every corner of Vermont who are involved in one of the many phases of agriculture, including dairy, beef, sheep, goat, horse breeding, cheese making, logging, sugaring, and so on.

The country's first government study profiling female farmers was released in January 1985. This report showed that nationwide 128,000 women, or 5.2 percent of the nation's farmers, were the sole or primary operators of their farms. In Vermont, however, 8.1 percent of all farmers were listed as women. That's 520 women, and it placed Vermont as sixth highest in the nation for women in agriculture.

Now take a look at this: the census of 1997 revealed that more than 782 Vermont women, or more than 13 percent, operate Vermont farms. According to Reenie DeGeus of the Vermont Agriculture Department, that's an increase of almost 8 percent in twelve years. Martha Izzi, who has a sheep farm in Shrewsbury, also does research about farm women. She has found that, nationally, women are the fastest-growing group buying small farms. Among those women the largest percentage going into agriculture are women couples. She says that in ten years 75 percent of American farmland will be owned by women. Well, these Granny Landlords do live longer, but the question is, who are they going to pass the land on to if there is no one in the family to run the farm? I know myself it is tough to find someone to operate our farm, and what's going to happen here in twenty years? Not everyone has the commitment and the know-how to farm.

When asked the question, "What does the word *farmer* bring to mind?" a majority of folks will say they see a male in blue bib overalls with a feed cap looking over a green meadow — maybe chewing on a long grass stem — a Grant Wood image.

"This farm, it's so beautiful. Cows, they come and go but the land will always be here. I put so many hours of labor into it, what a sense of accomplishment I have when I work on it.

"Some people look forward to weekends. Can you imagine that? I feel sorry for them. Why, every day is my weekend. Gosh, I wish I could start all over.

"Commitment!" Gert yelled it out as if it was a patriotic slogan. "Sole commitment, that's what farming is. I can't remember taking a vacation ever! We do what we want! We're the boss! We're free!"

— Gert Lepine, *Vermont People*, 1990

I confess I've been guilty of this vision myself even after spending a lifetime farming with my family on our Jersey farm, but after seeing those statistics and reading this book, my vision of the male farmer is fading as fast as the snow disappears in April.

A majority of the farmers in this book are not Vermonters by birth or by chance but almost exclusively by choice. The state of Vermont appears to be

a Mecca beckoning individuals with a dream to fulfill. Vermont has the raw materials to make these dreams a reality.

When it comes to natural beauty, Vermont has got it all! The mountains, the rivers and valleys; the lakes and small ponds that I now love to fish; the varieties of bird life and wild animal life; the thousands of acres set aside as public land for everyone's enjoyment, the sense of privacy, of space, of being your own boss; what more could you ask?

The four seasons are very distinct in Vermont, although summer sometimes seems cheated of a couple months! Who doesn't enjoy the vibrant colors of autumn followed by the exciting snowfalls of winter with occasional thaws that remind us that spring is just around the corner with its sugaring season, as the good earth comes to life once more!

Vermont still has available smaller plots of land waiting to be pioneered into a workable lifestyle. Traveling the back roads of the state is really revealing. You never know what you'll find just around the corner — maybe a family with a lifestyle you envy and admire!

My writing has just been interrupted by the latest news on a local television station about an already large farm operated in Bridport that plans to expand to 1,100 cows. In Charlotte another farm family hopes to merge their numerous farms into one big outlay of buildings that could house 2,500 cows. Needless to say, the neighbors are not happy about the expansion, but it could be worse. In Idaho there are farms with 12,000 cows in a mile radius, and neighbors who live nearby sometimes wear gas masks.

In sharp contrast are Vermont small-farm operators that are diversifying and doing intensive farming on limited acreage. As an example, sheep, which were Vermont's major domestic animal at the beginning of the 20th century, went into almost nonexistence and in the past twenty-five years has made a strong comeback with the raising of lambs for meat, making cheese from the milk and even soaps that are sold at specialty shops and local farmers' markets.

"Goat milk is in demand for cheese and as a health food drink. Did you know that it is naturally homogenized? What is happening in Vermont is that small-farm operations are proliferating. They are keeping the land open, which attracts tourism.

They supply fresh food to their neighbors and region. They make the soil fertile and the small plot farmers are against the use of chemicals. What they do is keep Vermont what it has always been, a small community of people whose sense of their state is mountains, valleys, green fields, and small farms. Perhaps this statistic is overlooked by those people who think of farming as agribusiness, but 90 percent of the dairy farms in Vermont consist of 100 cows or less.

These are the herds that photographers search out and are pictured grazing on green rolling pastures with a nearby red barn. Are the large, box-store-type dairy farms really that appealing as a tourist attraction? Have you ever seen a dairy herd grazing in the Champlain Valley? They are kept for most of their short life in stalls, where they are fed and milked. This is called concrete grazing.

My thanks and best wishes go out to these Vermont women farmers. Their stories are inspiring; their courage is admirable. Furthermore their role in the future of Vermont agriculture, and their role as models for the rest of the country in creating small, community-based farms, is of utmost importance. Vermont is nurturing another revolution.

GERT LEPINE
Morristown, Vermont

Introduction

The idea for this book came to me in the spring of 1995 somewhere in Arkansas. I was driving back from the Texas Panhandle after taking photographs and doing research for the book *People of the Great Plains*. I had photographed and interviewed a number of cattle ranchers who were women. They were tough, competent, and I liked them; the photograph of one of them, Margaret Hawkins from Arthur, Nebraska, became the cover.

I had decided to do a book on ranch women until I saw *Hard Twist*, by Barbara Van Cleve (University of New Mexico Press). This is a book on ranch women by a woman who spent her life in the saddle with a camera, and it is such a good book there was no sense for me to do another.

So I said to myself, driving across Arkansas, what shall I do? American farm women? No, too broad a subject; the logistics would be a nightmare. New England farm women? Hmmm. Not enough pizzazz. Vermont farm women? Well, I live in Vermont and I already know a number of them. I thought of the Lepine sisters, and then I recalled Rowena Austin and May Dutton, the first farm women I met in Vermont, when I was a teenager.

When I finally returned to Vermont, I began to collect farm women names from friends and county farm agents. I did the first interviews and photographs in 1998. As so often happens on my personal projects, I ran out of money and devoted myself to paying projects, including the book *The First Time I Saw Paris*, published by Random House. I returned full time to the farm women project in late 2000 and spent much of the next two years in the field meeting farm women, interviewing and photo-

graphing them, writing, editing, and working in the darkroom.

When I became deeply involved in this book, traveling the length of Vermont and sleeping in my Air Stream camper in farmers' pastures, I began to question just what I was doing. These farm women were talking about issues much broader than Vermont. They were concerned about caring for animals, working as a family unit, keeping the land open. They were against the use of pesticides and chemical fertilizers. They sold their produce locally and regionally and railed against the use of fossil fuels to transport fresh produce thousands of miles. They believe state and federal bureaucracies are too directed to agribusiness and CAFOs (confined animal feeding operations), which are, in essence, factories. They dislike large farms, and to make up for lack of size they are diversifying what they produce and increasing the return per acre.

Above all they relish being their own boss while working the earth. I found them to be passionate in their beliefs and so very dedicated.

This book is about small farms serving their communities and in some cases their neighboring states. It is about keeping Vermont an agricultural state on a personal and community level. It is also about the small-farm movement pushed by Vermont women that started in this state and has already spread to Maine, Pennsylvania, and even to the West Coast.

Let's take a look at some of the foods Vermonters buy in grocery stores. Take a bunch of carrots grown in California. You buy them cheaper at the local supermarket than you buy a bunch that is locally grown, but those California carrots are often grown

on desert land irrigated through state and federal subsidy programs. Aquifers are being lowered, sometimes drastically. Pesticides and herbicides are used liberally. The produce is shipped by truck to eastern distribution warehouses where the carrots are repacked into another truck and delivered to the local stores. Along the way the trucks use a lot of diesel fuel. How much fuel does it cost? I don't know, but ten liters of orange juice need a liter of diesel fuel for processing and transport; to produce a bushel of corn it takes 1.2 gallons of fuel oil; to bring a 1,000-pound steer to market consumes 284 gallons of fuel oil. Let's not talk about all the subsidized repairs to the interstate highways. These carrots (the average fresh food product travels 1,800 miles before it reaches the shelf) are not good for the environment, and, as a chemically enhanced product, it just might not be good for your family. And it also may put local farmers out of business. In 1910 the average farmer received 44 cents of very dollar spent at the retail store — the same amount as was spent on marketing. In 1990, the farmer received 9 cents of every dollar, but the marketing costs went up to 67 cents per dollar. So who is paying for the endorsements on a box of cereal?

Let's talk about subsidies. There is a new $180 billion farm bill passed by Congress and signed by President Bush. From that bill the U.S. government spends $2 billion a year subsidizing the American cotton growers (average net worth, $800,000), and they have doubled their production in the past twenty years so there is a glut on the market. Meanwhile, Vermont dairy farmers have seen the cost of milk drop from $15.80 a hundredweight in

2001 to $13.80 for the first six months of 2002, and the price is dropping every month.

America, the Common Market, and Japan spend $350 billion a year to subsidize the agricultural products in their countries. The United Nations figure these farm subsidies cost poorer countries about $50 billion a year in lost agricultural exports. What happens to poor farmers in a country where they cannot sell their products? Their families suffer economically. There is little money to provide education and health care. If their children live to become adults, would you think that maybe they would be inclined to hate countries like America?

Let's take another look at a statistic. Only 8 percent of the country's farms produce 72 percent of the national harvest. This is where the subsidies go. Agribusiness is concentrating so quickly that in the near future our global retail food system may be controlled by five or six firms — in America perhaps it will be WalMart. Such concentration will force suppliers to sell at low margins and simplify their product line. Diversity in products is not a choice: 90 percent of all commercially produced turkeys — in the world — come from three flocks. That makes a uniform product, but the reduced genetic diversity usually means weakened immune systems and strong doses of antibiotics.

So why fight it? *Why not?* And that's what the small-farm movement, and the farm women of Vermont and America, are involved in. They have some help. The Vermont Agriculture Department works hard at marketing out of state (but fall flat on their face in supporting small farms, although their grunts — their field people — are usually respected by farmers). There is the Fresh Food Network, which brings farmers and chefs together so the restaurants have fresh produce on their menus. Lydia Ratcliff's Fancy Meats from Vermont and Vermont Quality Meats bring fresh, unfrozen whole animals to some of the best restaurants in America, from Boston to New York City. The Slow Food Movement, started in Italy, now has 60,000 American members. It's an answer to the fast-food world, of course; the association is dedicated to exposing people to the best regional food and cooking. One of their projects is to save four original species of the American turkey, one of the few domestic animals originating in the Americas.

Glynwood Center of Cold Spring, New York, is a nonprofit organization specializing in community stewardship. They have a new program called Smart Agriculture, Connecting Communities, Farming and Food. The program directs a community to develop a sustainable agricultural base. Glynwood Center is also involved in building a permanent and large farmers' market building to support regional farmers in Butler County, Pennsylvania. It could be a model for other farmers' markets in urban areas.

These are important steps in this small revolution. Much more can be done in Vermont. The Vermont Agriculture Department should invest in marketing fresh produce to urban markets in other states. The Vermont Land Trust in some cases provides a valuable service but needs to recognize that preserving Vermont's land is not all about money and selling development-protected land so they become hobby farmer estates; there need to be loan programs to enable young people to take over farms from older, retired farmers. Some of these farmers wonder just what will happen to their conserved lands when they die. More towns should develop a program to aid farmers. The small farm — their hay fields, pastures, and barns — are the backdrop that brings tourists who enrich the restaurants, lodges, and stores. A local sales tax that keeps land open would make sense to tourists and visitors, which the state's 9 percent meals tax does not.

Staying small. That is Vermont's future. After September 11 many Americans want to work at something with meaning and fulfillment and to some it is returning to a simpler life close to the land. The large farm subsidy pork passed by the government embarrasses many aware Americans. Environmental concern, not on the radar screen in Washington, is an acute issue with voters. The collapse of Enron and World Com and the duplicity of Anderson and other huge companies makes us wonder what happened to honesty. Does being big mean a corporation has the right to rip off their investors and tear up their employees' lives at the benefit of their executives? Is there a better way to handle our lives, our economy, our country, our environment?

Small farms and selling local to local is a way to respect the fact that we as a nation were built as individuals and personalities, not as corporate conglomerates. Vermont farm women are not even a blight on a blade of wheat in the agribusiness of America, but they are making us aware that there is something pretty good about being small.

PETER MILLER
Colbyville, Vermont

It was the summer of 1948 when my family moved from Connecticut into a small vacation home that my uncle owned in Weston, Vermont. My mother was divorced with little income, and at that time Vermont was an inexpensive place to live. To me, Vermont was Heaven — there were mountains and fishing streams and so few people. I could hunt, fish, and ski, and what more could a fourteen-year-old boy want? Our house sat on a small knoll on Piper Hill looking west. I could see, across the valley, a hillside farm with a large red barn and a cupola — one of the thirteen dairy farms in the town. I used to sit on the front lawn and gaze out at that farm. I remember thinking how relaxed that view was; the hay fields, the woods, and the red barn and house seemed to belong to each other, like a family.

Three years later my shotgun and rifles were stolen, and my mother gave me an insurance check for $160. I don't know why, but I bought a camera, an Ikoflex, which was a twin lens reflex. And so I began to shoot photographs, and it became, and still is, a compulsion and a career.

The subjects I chose to photograph were farm scenes, so of course I was drawn to the farm across the valley. The first time I met the Austins I walked up Morgan Hill, which we skied in the winter, climbed through a narrow strip of woods to a large maple isolated on a hill within a hay field, and then down through the pastures, up past a grove of apple trees to the farm. The barn lay next to a dirt road. On the other side was a wood-frame house with an ell and a long roofed porch. On the porch were two rockers. In one of them sat an elderly man with a full gray mustache. He was smoking a pipe. His eyes were

as blue as the August sky. Next to him was a woman who appeared to be from the past century. A long gingham dress came to her feet, on which she wore black, button-up boots, similar to Dr. Martens. Over the dress she wore an apron. Her hair was upswept, bunched in the back, and held with a comb. They looked at me curiously and Will nodded his head. Both were rocking back, and forth. I went up and said hello and we introduced ourselves. His name was Will Austin and next to him was his wife, Rowena. She gave me a big grin. With their wrinkles and Rowena's antique dress they appeared to be from another century, which they were — I found out later that Will was born in 1879; Rowena in 1882.

"You're one of those boys who moved into that chicken coop aren't you?" Will asked. Rowena put her had back and gave a big laugh. She had a missing front tooth.

Our home was modern with a big slanted front window made up of six panes. Yes, I thought to myself, it did look like a chicken coop.

For a while I just sat there while they rocked, saying little. Rowena went inside and brought out a cup of cold water. It was spring water, she said, from a well above their house. Will asked me if I wanted to see the barn, and we walked across the dirt road to the barn, opened the door, and I followed him in. Lined up in the soft barn light were his beautiful wagons and sleighs, which he drove into town with his Morgan.

I returned to the porch and asked if I could take some photographs.

"Oh no!" said Rowena, and she heisted up her dress and scurried into the house.

"I guess not," said Will. He kept smoking that pipe and rocking. He asked me where I was from and how old I was and where I was going to school. Rowena never reappeared.

As I was sitting on the front of the porch I sneaked a photograph of Will. I was fidgeting with

the camera and opened the case and held it in my lap pointing up toward Will in the rocker. It was a twin lens reflex, and the shutter made no noise.

On my next visit Will let me take some photographs of him, but Rowena — oh no. She would say hello, but when the camera came out she would flounce into the house.

I did photograph other Vermont farmers. I shot pictures of our neighbor Hugh Foster as he hayed near our home and of May and Cliff Dutton as they were gathering hay in a field near the West River, which flows through town. May Dutton was a slip of a woman with an impish grin. I would say she was approaching her seventies. She was pitching hay into a wagon. She also had bright blue eyes and her face and arms were as tan as an acorn. She always

wore a jumper with two straps going over her shoulders. One strap was always falling off, and I kept wondering when the jumper would slip off her thin and wiry body. Her eyes seemed to laugh when she told stories, such as the time she was leading the cows off the mountain one evening, and a catamount tracked her down to the barn. She would tell stories of bears and wild cats and scare the local children, and always she wore this impish grin and her blue eyes gleamed and her slip of a dress always seemed ready to fall off.

I had these pictures developed and made into small prints. I thought they were jewels, and I put them in envelopes into a drawer. These early negatives were stolen out of my Volkswagen in Greenwich Village in New York in the early 1960s.

It wasn't until 1959 — nine years later — that I came to know Rowena. I had graduated from Burr and Burton Academy in Manchester and from the University of Toronto and spent three years as a U.S. Army photographer in Paris, France. I was discharged in the fall (no good-conduct medal) and returned to Vermont. The house was empty — my mother was teaching in Italy, my sister was a PanAm hostess, and my brother was out West. I was thinking of my future, but not too seriously, and I took a job for the winter as a ski patrolman at Big Bromley in Peru, just 10 miles from my home. Ski patrolling is a wonderful way to enjoy a passion, but the winter of '58–'59 was light with snow and heavy with rain, temperature drops, wind, and ice. For two weeks in February I was laid off and stayed at home. There was not much to do, so I spent my time visiting the Austins across the valley. I went almost every day with my cameras I brought back from Europe, a Canon 35mm and a twin lens Rolleiflex.

The first time I was in their house was a surprise. The porch door led into the kitchen. To the right was a door that went to an outdoor shed where Will

Of course, you could listen in on these conversations, and Rowena didn't miss a word. She usually had a cat or two on her lap as she bent over, phone on her ear, a frown on her face as if she couldn't hear too well. The party line was the only town newspaper we had, and Rowena made the most of it. Once, when I was there, she was listening and suddenly blurted out in that strong deep voice of hers, "Now you know that isn't true at all!" And hung up the phone with a slam and a gleam of triumph for having the last word.

Rowena was a Shattuck who was born in the north end of town. Her father was renowned for making a cough medicine that was also taken when you didn't have a cough. She married Will, the son of Walter, and moved to the Austin farm overlooking the valley. Rowena was an outdoor woman who preferred to work in the fields and do barn chores. They only had seven cows that they milked, but they kept a bunch of young calves that Will sold in the fall. He also traded horses and once had pigs, and they kept chickens. There were two groves of apple trees, one in the fields below the house and one above the house. They had a number of varieties, some now called antique apples — Green River, Banana, Strawberry, and Jonathans. Rowena and Will would pick the apples, wrap each one individually in newspaper and store them in their cool cellar, along with potatoes and other root vegetables. Rowena would help with the milking and collect the eggs. Although she wanted to be haying, she had to cook for the hired hands and Will. One of the hired hands was Fred Johnson. He always wore a railroad cap and spoke in thees and thous if you listened carefully, for he also had a lisp and no teeth. Once he bought a pickup truck from his earnings with the Austins and other locals. He hitchhiked to Rutland to pick it up, and the salesman drove down to Weston with him to teach him how to drive. When they got to his home, a

kept the wood for their stoves and his tools. In the kitchen was a wood cookstove and under a back window was a lead sink piled with dishes ready to be washed. Next to it was a lead reservoir that was brimming with spring water that ran constantly. Above was a cupboard, and on the far wall an old poster calendar was pinned up. I think it had been there for about fifty years.

There were newspapers everywhere. Stacks of them. Magazines too. I noticed an agricultural magazine that was printed in 1917. It appeared the Austins threw nothing away. In the parlor off the dining room there were aisles through stacks of newspapers. One led to the stove, another led to Will and Rowena's chairs, and then to his rolltop desk and a squat iron safe. Another aisle led to their

bedroom. The old four-poster was layered with blankets, and there was a woodstove in the bedroom. The house hadn't been renovated since it was built in the 1800s and had no insulation, just lath and plaster.

Rowena had her own space in the dining room between the parlor and the kitchen. She sat in front of a window and talked on the telephone. I should say listened. At that time all of Weston's phones were on a party line. I don't know how many were on Will and Rowena's line but there were probably about eight families. Every person on the party line had their own ring. One long, and one short for the Austins, two longs for the Seeleys, one long and two shorts for Steve and Baird Hall, four longs for Charley and Betty Foster, and so on.

shack on the Moses Pond road, the salesman expected Fred to give him a ride back.

"By God no!" he replied. "Git back thyself."

Rowena was renowned as a cook and was famous for her muffins, potato pancakes, chicken, and apple and peach pies. She made doughnuts in strips, and then pinched the ends together. But she was a sloppy housekeeper; she really wanted to be outside and Will wanted a neat house. It was one of the differences they both learned to live with.

In the winter of 1959, when I visited, the Austins were mostly housebound. Will would sit in the rocker, smoking his pipe and falling asleep. He loved to tell stories and sometimes he recited poetry.

Rowena sewed when she wasn't listening in on the phone. The window light illuminated her work, and behind her was a wall clock with the wooden works that did not keep time — there was no need for that. She made some of her own clothes and patched everything. Once a friend visited in the summer and saw the laundry hanging outside. There was a set of Rowena's bloomers pegged to the line that she had sewn together from chicken feed bags. On the bloomers was the chicken feed logo, *Lay or Bust.*

She fussed with her cats. One of them she called Steamboat Coming Around the Bend, another was Chattanooga Choo Choo. She had about seven of them. When she went out for the mail she put on crumpled fedora, and, during the winter, she used a cane to keep from slipping on the ice and wore a denim coat over her gingham dress. She was regal, head in the air, like a figurehead on a four master, walking to the mail box and back, the cats scurrying around her.

When I visited we would talk for a while and then I would start taking pictures. Sometimes Will would nod off to sleep or walk to his rolltop desk and look at bills through a magnifying glass. Rowena would go on about her cats, laugh at some of their antics, sew, and always stay by the phone, waiting to listen in.

It finally snowed — big flakes were sifting down on a windless day when I photographed Will and Rowena outside, posed together with the barn behind them. The photograph would become, thirty-one years later, the cover of *Vermont People.* It was one of the few photographs of the Austins that I posed.

I went back to ski patrolling at Bromley, and that spring I left Vermont to work, for a short while, as an assistant to Yousuf Karsh, the photographer. Then I moved on to a job as a reporter for *Life* magazine. I realized I had to learn how to write. It was the last I saw of the Austins.

In the early 1960s Rowena developed sores on her feet. She had poor circulation and was taken to the Springfield hospital where she developed gangrene. They amputated one foot just below the knee. I heard she was a terrible patient, screaming at the nurses and complaining wickedly. She probably would have calmed down if she had a couple of her cats.

The only way Will would stay in the hospital with Rowena was if someone would stay with the cats. Alan Chalmers, now my brother-in-law, agreed to

house- and cat-sit and keep the woodstoves burning. Will was taken by friends to the hospital, and he and Rowena shared a room in a rest home.

Alan moved into the house and bought cat food at Parkhurst's store, the only store in Weston. In the winter they sold mostly root vegetables and some lettuce, all other food was canned. Many times the road was too slick with snow, and Alan couldn't make it up to the Austin house. He would have to park his car and hike 2 miles uphill from town. He lived in the Austin home most of the winter.

"I remember that there was an overhead cupboard door above the sink where the sugar and flour was kept," says Alan. "Every morning that door would be open, although I swear I closed it the evening before. I would close it again, and in the morning it would be ajar. This happened every night. I sprinkled flour on it to see if a mouse was getting in but in the morning there were no animal tracks. I just couldn't figure it out. I remember not being very comfortable in that house and was glad when that duty was over. This was about the time Rowena died."

Rowena died on May 6, 1962, in bed next to Will in the rest home. Early May is a bleak time in Weston, a time of sleet, snow, wind, and rain. After the funeral Will returned to his farm.

"I gave Will a bill for the cat food," Alan recalls. "He gave it a long read and looked at me with his keen blue eyes and said in soft voice, 'My, that is an awful lot of money for cat food. How much did you feed them?' I guess they always bought by the can."

Will lived alone in the house for almost a year. In May, just a year after Rowena died, a neighbor found Will inside his home, on the floor, leaning against the door; he had had a stroke and had been there all day. He rode in the ambulance that went up the steep hill that climbs Terrible Mountain and eventually leads to the Springfield Hospital. It is the last trip taken alive for so many of the older Weston natives; they come back in a coffin, to the cemetery

and her father raises sheep and chickens. At Weston island is another sheep farm on land Cap Woodcock used to hay.

I have a handcarved yoke in my home. I found it so many years ago split in two and lying on the ground behind the Austin barn. I took it home and glued it together, and whenever I look at it I have this image of Rowena trudging up the hill to the house with two buckets of milk slung from ropes suspended on either side of the yoke, that old fedora on her head, the gingham dress hiding her ample body.

The farm women on the following pages were interviewed and photographed between 1998 and 2002, but the journey in my soul began more than fifty years ago with the farm women and men I came to know and love in Weston.

at the foot of the hill, just north of Ken and Anna Walker's farm. Will died May 26, 1963, when the apple buds were in full bloom.

Will and Rowena are buried in the town cemetery, along with other farming couples — Cliff and May Dutton and her impish smile, Hugh and Rachel Foster, Charlie Foster — his wife will be along pretty quick. So will Ken and Anna Walker. There are no more dairy farms in Weston, although my niece, Carrie Chalmers, has a flower and vegetable farm

Rosina Wallace — *Dairy Farmer* — WALLACE FARM

Rosina Wallace cups her hands over her mouth, lifts her face toward the pasture and hay fields that slope up to the afternoon sun, and lets out with a call of "Here Boss!" Her voice reverberates over the 225 acres of her farm, and the Jerseys in the upper pasture — "my critters," she calls them — line up and head down the cow path to the barn. It's time for milking.

In the evening, she wanders the upper pasture, searching for a calf she suspects one of her cows has dropped in the woods. From the pasture there is a magnificent view of blue-hazed mountains — Mt. Mansfield to the north and the Worcester range looming across the valley from her Waterbury farm. She walks the hedgerow of birch and cherry trees

that shade a stone wall and then follows a cow path that twists into the woods. After a few minutes of searching, she finds the afterbirth, but no calf.

"Once a calf was born and didn't come out for two days. It was feeding on its own . . . one smart calf to avoid the coyotes."

Rosina spots one of her barn cats prowling the stone wall, hunting chipmunks. "You stay up here," she warns the cat, "and the coyotes will get you."

Overhead the repetitive call of snipes echoes down, a noise made by the wind whistling through tail feathers. The birds are barely visible as they swoop and soar in their aerial mating dance.

"Mr. Snipe, you are having a lot of fun up there." Snipes appear in the sky on the first evenings of

summer. In the early-spring twilight when the snow is bleaching into grass, woodcocks yo-yo up and down in their mating flight. In late summer after haying, red-tailed hawks circle the fields looking for mice.

Rosina passes an outcropping of rock in the hay field that has been there forever — she played there as a child while her father hayed — and follows the tractor trail down to the barn. From her rubber boots up to her denim jacket, Rosina appears trim but sturdy. On hot days a straw hat filters sun through the weave and flecks her face with sunlight. Like her eyes, her curly hair is dark, and she's more often smiling than not; there's a healthy sensuality and energy within this farmer. She looks a lot happier than her great grandmother Lavinia

Wallace. "For 136 years the Wallace family has worked this hillside farm, and it has been the Wallace women, for the most part, who kept the farm going," says Rosina, who has a copious scrapbook of photographs.

"Sidney and Lavinia Wallace bought the farm in 1866, but Sidney was such a poor money manager they probably would have lost the farm if Lavinia hadn't had such a tight hold on the purse strings.

"Then their son, my grandfather, James Wallace, ran a good farm with fruit crops, maple sugaring, cows, chickens, and pigs, but he died in the flu epidemic of 1917. Grandmother Florence used the insurance money to pay off the mortgage. She was a little woman, but she kept the farm going and all seven of her children graduated from college.

"Only my father, Keith, came back to the farm after college, when he married my mom, Gladys. I grew up doing chores and then went to college. I was teaching in Lyndonville when Dad asked me if I wanted to farm, as he was going to run for the Vermont Legislature. I quit teaching and came back to the farm in 1980."

In the years since, Rosina has remained a single farmer, and she watched Waterbury change from an agricultural community to a bedroom town. When she was a child there were seven farms etched on the hillside across the valley that she could see from her hay fields and pastures, and she knew the families who lived there. Now there are two farms left and more houses than you can count.

"I'm just hanging on," she says. The barn is old, bent with generations of frost heaving the foundation, and the red paint is cracked and faded. An ancient Ferguson tractor, as worn as the barn, is parked in the back, facing uphill. This is old-fashioned farming, where the milkers go out every day to pasture during the summer instead of being kept in a free-stall barn.

"Farming is tiring and hard work, but I grew up on this farm. I love the view almost as much as scratching a cow behind the ears, but I wouldn't farm if I had to farm anywhere else. This place is free and clear, with no mortgages. Developers offer more money than I can imagine for my property, but I won't sell. This is roots, it's family, and I think it is an okay thing to do, to feed people, in spite of the fact they don't appreciate it because they think food comes from a grocery store. I am a Yankee Vermonter. I am high blooded. I have the right to be. I was born to be. So I prefer to hold on to this farm as long as I can."

In the summers, Rosina has city kids come up to live with her, and often schoolchildren come to visit.

"A busload of kindergarten kids came to the farm from Montpelier and watched me take the cows to pasture, and later I asked them if they had any ques-tions and this kid looked up at me and asked, 'Where's the farmer?'" Rosina shakes her head and smiles just a bit. "I had to explain that women can be farmers too."

The old farmhouse doesn't look like it has been remodeled. The kitchen is simple with a large wooden table in the center. On one end of the room sits the wood cookstove and the door to a large

pantry. In the living room is an organ and photos on the wall of five generations of Wallaces who have lived on this farm

Keith, Rosina's father, was respected as a farmer, legislator, and storyteller. He taught his daughter how to raise calves, care for a sick cow, make the soil more productive, and survive on very little. Most important, he taught her to keep her cows healthy, although he wasn't that healthy himself.

He suffered terribly from arthritis, and by 1964 it was so bad in his back that he was eating twelve aspirins a day. In 1985 his wife, Gladys, died of diabetes. And ten years later, Keith was diagnosed with a bleeding ulcer.

"It was probably the darned aspirin and coffee he drank," Rosina says. "He used to scoop cream out of the milk cooler for his coffee. He had angina, and when he was eighty-six his body just totally wore out. He had cataracts and couldn't hear much anymore, and he developed asthma and an awful cough. His kidneys were failing and so were his lungs. The last twenty-four hours he wasn't sure where he was anymore. We had rented a hospital bed, and it was obvious that it didn't feel like home to him.

"Finally that morning I said, 'Dad, do you want to sit in your chair by the kitchen stove?'

"'Can I?' he asked.

"'Sure,' I said. 'We can carry you out and you can sit in your chair.'"

Rosina looks out across her fields toward her pastures.

"He died sitting in his chair because he felt he was home. That was the second of June, 1995."

Too many cows," said Maggie, who works the midnight shift at the Nop Farm near Middlebury. By morning she will have milked 340 Holsteins. She examines any sick cows in the herd of 450. She tallies milk production for each cow, does pregnancy checks and shots, and oversees the balance of their feed.

This is modern farming, where the only cows that graze a pasture are heifers and those that are dry. The milkers live twenty-four hours a day in narrow stalls in a long, shedlike barn. Some call this type of farming concrete grazing. Like most American businesses, the bottom line for the larger farms (and Nop Farm is a relatively small one) is efficiency — produce more milk at less cost per gallon.

"Here a cow only has two or three years of production and it is done," says Maggie. "It bothers me a lot to see them go. I care for animals. I love my work. I like everything about a farm. If I had my way I would be back on a small farm."

But she isn't, and the reason is because of her sex. Maggie grew up on a six-generation family farm in a nearby valley, split by the Middlebury River and bordered by the Otter Creek. The river-bottom soil is rich and fertile. They had a 150-cow Jersey herd and a 2,000-tap sugarbush.

"As a little girl I enjoyed working with cows and sugaring. From my father I learned to love the land."

Maggie never wavered in her enthusiasm to be a farmer, but the skill she learned was never acknowledged by her father. Her brother managed the farm, and it went into debt and her father took out a mortgage to save it. A barn fire crushed thirty-five cows. A sister and brother-in-law moved back to the farm,

but that did not work out. Maggie entered into partnership with her father and brother to operate the farm.

"It was not going well," Maggie recalls. "I wanted to buy out the farm, but my father decided on my brother. He never saw what I was capable of. So I was out.

"It was like a death for me. I loved that place. Just loved it."

"Why did your father decide on your brother?" I ask her.

"Because he was his son."

Eventually the bank foreclosed and the Seeley Farm was no more.

"Well, life goes on," says Maggie. She now lives in a house with a nice garden and shade trees that is surrounded, on the summer I visited, by high rows of corn — an oasis.

"I was hired to work on an organic dairy farm and that barn burned and the farm was sold. Then I had so many offers from other farmers to manage their herds. I had my pick."

The farm community recognizes Maggie as one of the best dairy herd managers in Central Vermont. Still, there are those who do not believe a woman's place is managing a big farm.

"Oh yeah, there's a lot of prejudice against women running a farm. Men, often salesmen, come in and ask to talk to the boss.

"'Well,' I reply, 'you're looking at the boss.'

"'Yes, but I mean, uhhh . . .' and they look at me dumbfounded.

"'You gotta deal with me.'

"In this job, if you're a woman, you have to

prove yourself twice over to men, but if you're good, boy, they will praise you up and down. It's a double standard."

Maggie has opened the door; now two other women have been hired at the Nop Farm to work with calves and heifers and help with the milking

Maggie's fight for recognition has cost her. The conflict during her years on the family farm and her lack of recognition as a farmer led to clinical depression.

"I had it off and on for seven or eight years. I found the right therapist and I decided against pills. I used to keep everything in, but now I just blurt it out. My mother gave and gave, and my father didn't give an inch. You know, I never was married, never wanted it, but my attitude has changed. I am fifty-five and I would like to meet somebody now."

Although she has been free of depression for thirteen years, Maggie sees a holistic healer and has learned to shed the negativity that she says does no good for body or mind.

"I've learned to communicate in different ways with people and myself, and I understand a lot more with animals. I listen to my gut. I'm my own person, and, yes, I take pride in what I've done. And in myself."

Debbie Landauer and Rebecca Moyer — *Garlic Gardeners* — THE NORTHERN PRIZE GARLIC COMPANY

As a journalist I was trained to be suspicious of coincidences. And yet . . .

Debbie Landauer and Rebecca Moyer did not know each other when they both moved to Vermont from Maine, where they had met their husbands, both teachers. Each became pregnant and had twins, about eighteen months apart. They love to garden. And both eventually moved to northern Vermont because it was too expensive to buy a home elsewhere in the state. Rebecca, Dave, and their twins live in Fairfield; while Debbie, Tom, and their twins reside in nearby Enosburg.

Finally *(inevitably?)*, they met. Destined, perhaps, to weave together their similarities, they created the Northern Prize Garlic Company and began to grow strains of the pungent and flavorful root that would thrive in this tough northern climate. They sell their crop locally and by mail order.

Rebecca, tall and loose limbed, has a glint in her eyes that hints of comic wildness. She studied horticulture in Long Island, where she grew up. During the summer she works on the farm of the correctional facility in St. Albans. During the winter she is involved in Community Action programs.

"I moved north because I didn't like the way Long Island was changing. The people weren't connected with farms; they did not know the names of plants or birds. I love physical work and find it exciting to watch plants grow. On a good year it is *so* much fun to pull out a garlic that has been in the ground only nine months and . . . 'WOW! Look at this big one!'"

Debbie is shorter, with an inquiring mind; a nascent activist. Trained as a teacher, she home-schools her two children, now ten, and raises vegetables and fruit for her family's table. She is the spokesperson for the company and its philosophy about food.

"I like the idea of having fresh food and knowing where it comes from. Rebecca and I have separate gardens, but we both grow organically. As our gardens expanded, our awareness of the overuse of chemicals and pesticides by agribusinesses also grew. And as a nation we shouldn't depend on fossil fuels to ship food around the country. Yet the U.S. Agriculture Department wants to get rid of the small family farm, and even here in Vermont the state promotes the marketing of fancy food to out-of-staters rather than

foster food self-sufficiency among Vermonters. Now the word *organic* has been federalized and the costs are so high that we can't afford to be certified, although we follow the organic precepts.

"It's time for all of us to be more self-sufficient. This is counter to the global marketplace, but I think it's much more sensible to eat locally."

Debbie and Rebecca support this belief with their own shopping. Whenever possible they buy local produce, expanding to New England and New York and then the entire East Coast if necessary. They find this difficult because 50 percent of food products sold in supermarkets is from the West and South. They believe New England could be self-sufficient, despite the northern climate. Their beliefs and actions are at the forefront of a movement that began in Vermont and is moving to other regions of the country.

"If there is no connection between the farmers and the people they feed, then there is no trust. We are building trust," adds Debbie.

They are certainly going at it in small bits. Northern Prize Garlic produces 600 pounds of garlic a year and has a couple of hundred customers.

They sell all they raise and say they can produce no more without hiring outside help. The garlic is planted in prepared beds and is in the ground nine months before it is harvested in the fall. It is then dried in a shed and then Debbie and Rebecca clean each bulb with a toothbrush, so there is no dirt or grit on them. It is a labor-intensive crop. "We call it Vermont panache," says Debbie.

Debbie and Rebecca net about $3,000 a year, which they put back into their property, following

their precept of using the land to pay for the land.

Of the four hundred strains of garlic in the world, Northern Prize Garlic grows twenty. Some are called "hard necks" and have large cloves with a mellow taste. They are best roasted; they don't keep well. "Soft necks" have smaller bulbs and are more pungent. They last longer and are used in garlic braids.

About six years ago Debbie and Rebecca had a garlic-tasting party where everyone wrote down their comments on varieties. Some of the descriptions are quoted in Northern Prize Garlic's catalog: *Lorz Italian* "is sweet and hot with an understated dignity"; *Nootka Rose* "hits the back of the throat with a benevolent vengeance"; *Persian Star* has a "bold, emphatic taste"; *Chesnok Red* is "crunchy, rich and mellow, with a nicely tapered shape."

Long used as a remedy for arthritis, recent studies show that garlic is effective against coronary heart disease, bronchitis, influenza, and colds. The medical journal *Antimicrobial Agent and Chemotherapy* recently reported that when allicin, garlic's main biologically active component, is released by cutting or crushing garlic cloves, it may alleviate cholesterol, retard tumor growth, disable dysentery-causing amoebas, and in some cases be used as an antibiotic to ward off infection. And some believe it has the same effect on vampires and the Devil.

But of course it's the flavor of the stuff that keeps the phone ringing at Northern Prize Garlic.

Barbara Eastman — *Farm Wife* — Eastman Farm

Why did I come to Vermont? I really don't know why . . . I was impelled, really, although I had never been here or met anybody from Vermont. It seems obvious to me now that my destiny was waiting like an invitation I had only to accept."

Sitting in the their living room, luminous on this summer day, Barbara explains her journey that ended on this 300-acre Addison dairy farm, in this house, with her growing family. Her large eyes are windows to her story, told cleanly, reflecting her discipline with words.

"In April of 1995 I just got it into my head that I had to go somewhere — leave Minneapolis — and do something. I'd never been east of Michigan, but I knew that was the direction I wanted to go. I talked about this need to take a trip and people asked me where I was going, so one day I just said, 'I'm going to Vermont.'

"And they said, 'Have you ever been there?'

"And I said, 'No.'

"So I thought I should ask somebody I knew who had gone to Middlebury College what Vermont was like.

"'Well, ummm, there are cows and there is skiing.'

"'I like cows,' I thought to myself. 'I'll check it out.'

"Maybe it was a night I spent with a farm family in Minnesota in 1990. That was my first inkling that farming was not some far-off alien enterprise. I never quite caught the success fever the way my college friends did, and it seemed ludicrous to me that they thought farmers were stupid when they knew how to do things we didn't know how to do.

"I arrived in Burlington, took a hotel room, and was looking for work when I saw a newspaper ad that read, 'Help wanted milking cows. No experience necessary.'

"I called them and said I liked cows but never worked with them and if they gave me a chance they wouldn't have to pay me for the first couple weeks. We had an interview, and after a few days they hired me and I had housing for me and my dog. It was really hard work but I liked it.

"Mike was an expert on rotational grazing and came to visit and consult the farmer I was working for, and I was immediately smitten. We were married the following year.

"The night before I was married I lay awake wondering if I was going to spend the rest of my life cleaning house and working really hard and not having a lot of fulfillment. You know I married into the farm; Mike already had a working farm. How was I going to operate without feeling like an employee? I didn't want to be in charge of anything. Some farm couples work it out by saying, 'I'm in

charge of milking. You're in charge of the field work,' or 'I'm in charge of the house, and you're in charge of the barn.' I had to be reassured that I was not an underdog, that I was not a lowly subservient wife, and that he welcomed me as an equal.

"So it was Mike who had the radical idea that we should be equals. He solved it in that common sense way Vermonters have when he said, 'I just want to be equal. I don't want to tell you what to do, and I don't want you to tell me what to do.' It made so much sense.

"I am more of a farm wife than a farmer's wife because I am married as much to the farm as I am to Mike. If something ever happened to Mike, I would want to continue farming. I guess cow shit just flows in my veins. I love to be outdoors. I like physical work. I like animals. I like to incorporate the physical and mental work as much as I can. Being self-employed is very important to me

"It's hard farming as a young mother. When John, our first child, was a baby we had so much work to do and he never slept, and there were nights I was so tired I could barely walk up the stairs. At the same time, I'm home with him and now his brother and our new baby, and it's nice to be doing meaningful work with them around so they can see what goes into our business and to understand what we do. As a family it is so important to work and play together. How many families get to do that anymore? Kids are separated from their parents and from their parents' work. I think it's hard for parents to go off to work all day and then come home and their kids have no understanding of what they have been doing all day. There's a better life for a family."

The barn, white frame house, and shed are tethered to a hump of land above a long curving driveway that cuts through pasture and hay fields, broad and treeless. Just barely visible behind the farm is the outline of Snake Mountain. The sullen

weather of the day before was swept south by cirrus clouds forming over Lake Champlain, and the light now is sharp and cattle are chasing each other in the far pasture. Barbara walks down the curving driveway to the fields where Mike is haying and where she'll drive a tractor, towing tightly packed hay wagons. She wrote me about it six months later:

The beauty of that day, and the peaceful feeling of being on the tractor made me think of Wendell Berry's poem "The Peace of Wild Things" and this should have been my answer of why I am here. His poem was sort of a mantra to me, on my trip from Minnesota, and I remember reciting it as I drove, sometimes enjoying the trip and other times wondering what in the hell I was doing. Anyway, I didn't leave Minnesota or come to Vermont because of his poem but I do think it was because of it that I recognized where I wanted to be, once I had arrived. I wanted to share it with you.

The Peace of Wild Things

When despair for the world grows in me
And I wake in the night at the least sound
In fear of what my life and children's lives may be,
I go and lie down where the wood drake
rests in his beauty on the water,
    and the great heron feeds.
I come into the peace of wild things
who do not tax their lives with forethought
of grief. I come into the presence of still water.
And I feel above me the day-blind stars
waiting with their light. For a time
I rest in the grace of the world, and am free.

from *The Selected Poems of Wendell Berry*, Copyright © 1998 Wendell Berry.

Laini Fondiller — *Goat Cheese Maker* — Lazy Lady Farm

The mountains of Westfield, 10 miles south of the Canadian border, curve and flow into each other, a collage that changes personalities by the season — during a summer rainstorm they are smoke colored and ethereal; chalk blue in November's soft light under leaden, snow-stuffed clouds; brutishly monochromatic on a cold winter day. Cedars grow in the valleys, and in the hills small blocks of pasture are just barely holding their own against an aggressive woods of beech, maple, poplar, birch, and ash.

Lazy Lady Farm is hidden in these mountains, tucked into the edge of the woods at the end of a sliding dirt road. Laini Fondiller, her partner, Barry, twenty-five goats, eight sheep, and a couple of dogs and cats live here. She is small limbed, almost fragile in appearance. Don't be fooled. She's a spit-fire and one of the first to sell Vermont farmstead goat cheese (the milk and cheese are produced on the same farm) that are winning national prizes.

Laini was in college in Indiana when she visited a farm for the first time and decided on the spot she would spend her life outdoors working the soil and raising animals — no indoor work for her. She worked on dairy and a pig farm in Massachusetts but realized something was missing. "What else is out there?" she asks. "I didn't feel comfortable with the future of dairying and didn't have the money to fund it." After talking to some friends that knew the French countryside, Laini took off for France.

She worked on a dairy farm and as a shepherd in the French alps. Then, through a classified ad in a French agricultural magazine, she found a job on a goat farm high in the mountains of central Corsica, a region better known as a hideout for bandits than

as goat country. "They made a beautiful cheese from a recipe handed down in the family. It was ripened four weeks in a cave and maggots grew on the rind. Everyone knew this. We would scrape down the rind, wrap it, and sell it throughout Corsica. It won gold prizes."

After two and a half years Laini was kicked out of France (she had no work permit) and returned to Vermont to work as a herdswoman on dairy farms. "It was the late 1970s and it was tough — brutal.

There were not many women farmers, and you had to prove yourself. My bosses kept me out flat, and I guess that turned me into a chore master myself."

Out of her $150 paycheck per week she saved $125 and in a few years had $20,000 saved, which she planned to invest in a small farm. She met Barry, a carpenter who had some land, and they moved on to his property and he built a barn. The first year she paid her way with a vegetable garden. The second year she bought a goat and made her

21

first batch of farmstead cheese. On her first day at the local farmers' market she made $15.

"This was in 1987. Most Vermonters would not taste goat cheese. They thought it was an awful idea, like shit on a shingle. It just wasn't eaten."

Laini persevered and increased her herd. She milked by hand and made the cheese in her kitchen. Slowly her tangy, distinctive cheese attracted a fan club and she began making different styles of goat cheese, all based on French recipes.

Then inspectors from the Vermont Agriculture Department shut down her cheese making. It was okay to make cheese in 5-gallon batches and pasteurize it at home in your kitchen, and do it in a home off the grid, they told her, but you can't sell it. To be certified Laini would need to purchase a pasteurizer and build a modern cheese plant to comply with regulations.

"We didn't see eye to eye," says Laini, which is her way of saying a battle was pending. "I was working out of my kitchen and selling cheese, and the state said no more will you do that."

Laini is a never-give-up scrapper. She testified about making cheese on a small scale and that it was as sanitary as large-scale cheese factories. At one meeting she quoted from a State of Vermont pamphlet.

"'At the turn of the century (1900), four million pounds of farmstead cheese were made in Vermont.' Now we are down to none," she said. "What have you done?" Laini was making cheese the way cheese was made one hundred years ago, because at the time their home had no electricity.

"I told state officials it was my constitutional right to farm this way. I got a pro bono lawyer from Rural Vermont (a lobbying group), and we had a public hearing and about fifty people came to testify in my behalf and I gathered 250 signatures. They were my customers from the farmers' market and were very loyal, but the Agriculture Department was filled with cow people, and goats and sheep were, and are, not high on their agenda."

The newspapers and television reported on Laini's crusade to make and sell cheese from her farm, and the public responded; Vermonters love an underdog who takes on the bureaucracy. In this case, the state caved in and allowed her to make cheese in her home.

"I had to shame them," says Laini. "They considered me a health risk. How could I be a health risk when I was selling my cheese to someone I was looking in the eye? I can't do that and hurt people and their children."

Now there are thirty cheese makers in Vermont, and Laini turns out a dozen types of goat cheese, which are aged in her new, humidity-controlled cave built by Barry. Yes, her farm now has electricity and she uses a milking machine.

All of her cheeses have their pedigree from France; her Pyramid (earthy, creamy, good with a burgundy) and Tomme (dense, mild, smooth) cheeses have won national prizes in America. Laini still sells at the Montpelier Farmers' Market, but most of her cheese is distributed by wholesalers. Although she milks and makes cheese seven to ten hours a day for ten months of the year, she recently traveled to Northern Italy to learn how to make what is listed as an endangered food — Violina de Capo, a type of prosciutto made from the leg of a kid and aged for three to six months in a humidity-controlled cave. Laini has made a sample, which is now being aged and tested at the University of Vermont.

She learned this on a mountain in the French alps. "I was a shepherd, and I had to go high up a mountain to bring down three ewes with recently born twins and two singles; the weather had turned very cold. It was a two-and-a-half-hour hike and very steep. I put two lambs in my backpack and hung one over my neck and was walking down with three anxious mothers trailing behind me. Halfway down I had to stop and rest. I was laying on the ground, and the mothers were nursing their lambs. When finished, one little lamb walked over and curled up in my arms to sleep. I was her mother. I knew then I had to have sheep in my life, and I always will."

She also organized Part of Vermont, a group of twelve food producers, to make a sausage from beef, lamb, kid, and pork. When Part of Vermont applied for a grant from the Agriculture Department, they were turned down, although they would have been given a loan.

"I was told the money Part of Vermont would make is too scrawny and that the Agriculture Department is not in the welfare business! That's like a matador waving a red cape at a fighting bull in a Madrid *Corrida*."

Political challenges are Laini's avocation, but to keep her sanity she stays close to her farm and her first love, which is making cheese. Her outlook is more French than American, and that is perfection in the taste of natural food products. "I like people enjoying the food I make and the pleasure it brings them." She also enjoys her goats. "They have character," she says, but it is her sheep that she is most fond of and which she keeps for their wool, which she makes into rugs, hats, and mittens, and for her soul. "They have their own secret society," she confides, opening her eyes wide and almost whispering. "They may, or may not, let you in."

Debbie and Laurie Johnson — *Horse Breeder and Cattle Farmer* — Saga-Morgans

Laurie Johnson raises Morgans. Her sister Debbie and her husband, Don Moffit, manage the Angus and tend to the machinery. They live on a 200-year-old farm next to a back road in Shaftsbury. Tucked into the lower folds of West Mountain, its pastures sweep upward to a line of woods, held in check by a long and straight chestnut post fence. A cornfield is blocked into the field below the Shaker-built barn — 100 feet long and 42 feet in width, wedged into a hillside. A tunnel runs from the house to the bottom of the barn. Years ago, cream was sep-

arated in the kitchen and the skim milk was dumped into the tunnel and collected in a pig trough. The frame farmhouse looks used and comfortable. Mature maples shade the front and overlook a small pond. It's the type of farm you find on Vermont calendars.

Just a mile to the west as the crow flies is a patch-work of fields and farms, but they are all in New York State — Grandma Moses country. To the east lies the southern reach of the Valley of Vermont, a country suburbia of gentility that has not quite breached the hill above the farm. Some of their new

neighbors don't like farming. It stinks, they say. And it is dirty.

But the Morgans. Oh the beauty of the Morgan horse! All one has to see is Laurie, lean and wiry, highly concentrated, holding a lunge line as one of her Morgans trots in a circle around her — neatly picking up its legs, neck arched, head held proudly high, tail flowing. Such beauty, such athleticism, such vanity!

The Morgan is Vermont's state animal, as it rightly should be, for Justin Morgan brought an

extraordinary stud to the independent republic of Vermont in 1791. The stud was named Figure and could outrace and outpull just about any horse, and the stocky, shaggy-coated horse's ability to pass on its potent genes to its foals was phenomenal. Settlers headed west rode the Morgan. The First Vermont Cavalry, mounted only on Morgans, fought in the Civil War; only 200 of the 1,200 horses survived. (The First had a total of 392 officers and enlisted men who were killed or died of wounds, disease, or accidents. They lost 95 Morgans captured by Mosby's Raiders on April 1, 1863.)

The Morgan was the automobile for the 19th century, and the horse did utility service in the 20th century, particularly in Vermont.

"In 1948 the road past this house was not plowed,

and you needed a horse and cutter to get to town," says Debbie. "If you see a Vermont picture of a cutter being pulled by a horse, it usually is a Morgan."

The first Morgan foaled on the Johnson farm, known as Saga-Morgans, was in 1963. Before that, it was a chicken farm, which Debbie and Laurie's grandfather started in 1948 because he thought there was more money in chickens than in selling bonds on Wall Street, which was his primary vocation. (There wasn't.)

Over time, Debbie and Laurie realized that sales of Morgans are dependent upon a luxury economy and in a recession they found themselves saddled with too many Morgans, so they made a decision to replace their low-end horses with beef cows.

Now they have twenty Morgans and fifty cattle, which they call a mixed-Angus herd. The sale of Angus beef (which brings 15 cents more per pound than Hereford beef) helps balance the ups and downs of the pleasure-horse market.

Debbie and Laurie are college graduates with degrees in agriculture. Both made a conscious decision to return to the family farm.

"When I was at Cornell," says Laurie, " I remembered the barn and special places in the field and the things we did with our farm, while many other people at college were very cosmopolitan and had no sense of roots or a physical place to go home to. Hard work has been a family ethic and is the backbone of what we do. So I came home, as Deb did before me, and we've been working the farm ever since. First it was chickens, and then chickens and cows, and now it is Morgans and cows."

But for all the hard work they have put into their 200-acre farm, it is now an anomaly, and Laurie can become a bit heated about farming in Bennington County.

"All farmers know that farmlands are vanishing. We hate it and wonder what the future holds with less farmland available. Farmers are passionate about America producing its own food. Just the day before the Trade Center went down we had a conservation meeting, and the question posed was that if there was a disaster and transportation broke down and there was no local food, what will city people do?

"We farmers are under attack by the population, by environmental laws, by people wanting to build on our land. They are dictating how we should manage our farm in ways that are counterproductive to farming. Neighbors from Long Island never before smelled cow manure and do not like it, and they don't like slow tractors on the road. They don't like

pesticides and fertilizers whether we use them or not. They don't like farming because it is 'dirty' from their perspective. It's now at the point where our Conservation District is attempting to make farmers aware of their bad image with many of the new Vermonters.

"How can we defend our farm against growing communities of people who have different priorities than we do about land?"

And will Saga-Morgans withstand the cultural invasion of suburbia?

"We don't have a trust fund, and it is possible we may have to develop our farm just because we need the money," says Laurie. Deb, shy, earthy, a good mechanic, is quiet as her sister talks.

"We have a right to live. It is our investment, our retirement. Maybe, in the future, we could lease the property to someone who wants to farm. Our hope is not with Vermont but with our New York neighbors a few miles away. There it is all farms.

"Well, we could waste our lives worrying. Why build your life toward the end of it? We are still excited about what we are doing, and we have twenty years down the line."

Ann Day — *Guest Farm* — Knoll Farm

It was a Vermont custom, in the past century and a half, to plant in front of a new home two trees that would mature and mark the generations of the family who lived there. In the early 1900s, when the McLaughlin farmhouse was rebuilt over the old foundation, the owners planted eastern cottonwoods. The one that remains turned out to be a wolf tree; it outstripped its twin, stealing the sun and forcing it to die. The wolf tree grew powerfully — within half a century it was 18 feet in circumference, and Ann Day and her husband, Frank, could hold hands with their two young children and circle the tree.

Ann and Frank Day were trying out a secondhand Chevy when they drove up Bragg Hill and saw a For Sale sign in front of a very big tree. They stopped the car and, finding no one home, walked past the house and barn and up the hill to a knoll where the pastures slide down to the valley. Far below the Mad River, glistening in the sun, thread through hay fields, into Waitsfield, past the covered bridge and the church. To the east beyond the river mountains rise, fencing in a valley view from north to south. There is a great sense of peace here, on this knoll, overlooking Vermont.

Within a week they bought the 150-acre McLaughlin Hill farm and moved in with their two young children. It was August 27, 1957. Over the next forty-four years the tree's girth expanded to more than 22 feet. In the summer its 108-feet-high canopy shaded the house like a beach umbrella. Today the trunk is so deeply striated that you can bury a hand in its crevices, and the limbs are massive. The swing that hangs down from the lowest limb has a wooden seat that is just high enough so children feet do not touch the ground. The kids who ride it — and there have been generations of them — feel a sense of freedom as they pump themselves into a high parabola. To those who come as guests the cottonwood becomes a symbol of the farm; to

Ann it has been a source of strength during the very best, and very worst, years of her life.

The Days were escapees from New Hampshire, ski instructors in search of better slopes as found at nearby Mad River Glen, and later Sugarbush. Frank was a woodworker; Ann likes animals, writing, and photography.

That first summer they decided to make Knoll Farm a working farm where more than 50 percent of the income is from lodging. During a very busy fall they installed a furnace and insulated the house. They had a wood cookstove with water reservoirs and a Franklin stove, but there was no heat upstairs, which was okay; skiers in the late 1950s were a hardy bunch. The Days built ski trails leading down from their farm to the village of Waitsfield, where they installed a rope tow powered by a Buick engine. Children from neighboring towns were offered free skiing and instruction. On weekends the Days taught at Mad River Glen.

Soon Frank and Ann bought their first animal — a Jersey cow named Amber. Frank milked. They bought ponies and horses and Scottish Highlanders and pigs and chickens. They planted a large vegetable garden and raspberry patch and built a small pond. The skiers wanted to come back in the summer and some sent their kids.

"It was like going to Grandma's and having fun on the farm," says Ann. "We had a two-week summer camp, and Frank did the hiking and camping. We had riding and swimming. The kids helped in the milk house, and sometime four of them would be milking one cow. They helped with haying. At the same time we had older guests. It was a lot of fun."

Knoll Farm's livestock provided sausage and ham, pork roast and chops, steaks and roasts; canned vegetables and fruit came from the land. There were seven bedrooms and sometimes the Days had so many guests they slept on the kitchen floor with the dogs and cats until they built a small addition for themselves.

After chores and when the dishes were done, Ann and Frank would walk up through the pasture, well trimmed by the Scottish Highlanders and horses, on up to the knoll. They sat on a sloping rock that faced the valley, blue hazed in the summer evenings, the tips of the mountains tinged red with the last rays of sunlight. These were peaceful moments, and they talked sometimes of building a retreat in the woods, for people to meditate and enjoy the solitude of beauty.

In 1966, during the winter, when their house was filled with skiers, Frank had a breakdown and had to be hospitalized. Few knew that he suffered from a split personality and manic depression, something he coped with when he was younger and appeared to have beaten.

"We all get depressed, and some people just have the makeup to be seriously affected by this illness," says Ann. "It's from an imbalance in the brain. At the time Frank had it, the medication they gave him was Thorazine, but there were lots of side effects. Frank couldn't plan, and sometimes he had to be dressed."

Ann took over more duties and chores and so did their children. Friends pitched in. In the spring Frank came home from the hospital. He had his good moments and his bad ones. At one point he overdosed on sleeping pills. He was in and out of hospitals for four years.

Still, the ritual of doing farm chores became a salve.

"Milking was so good for Frank," remembers Ann. "He'd go out with his stainless-steel milk pail with warm water in it and wash the cow's teats and the udder and then, after washing out the pail, sit down on the metal milking stool. I can still hear the sounds. He'd sit there while I was taking care of the horses and start milking, and you could hear the ping of the milk in the pail and then the swish of it. He'd lean his head against her flank — Nelly was her name, and just milk away. Twice a day he would do that, and it was a quiet, peaceful time for him. Meanwhile the pig would be screaming for some milk, and the kittens sat around him while he was milking, waiting for a squirt in their faces, which they would lick off. And the froth built up in the milk pail. That was a good time. The other time Frank liked so much was driving the tractor and mowing the hay fields. These chores with a rhythm seemed to help."

July humidity and fast-moving cold fronts bring thunderstorms to the Green Mountains; they can be black and loud and so low you want to hide under the bed. Just such a storm struck the Mad River Valley on July 28, 1970, the day after Frank disappeared. No one really knows, but Frank probably walked up to the knoll with the wide view, turned his back on it, and strode into the darkness of the woods. The state police brought bloodhounds to search for him but with no luck. It was Alan and Mike, Ann's son and son-in-law, who found him the next day. They were riding their horses up the logging trail when Mike spotted him. Frank had killed himself.

Frank was buried on the knoll, and a granite tombstone was raised there. Two crossed ferns are carved on it. The stone is just high enough for a Scottish Highlander to rub its belly on. Not far away is a flat stone for a family dog, Tiba, who died in 1978. Their daughter Deb was married here, and Ann plans to be buried next to her husband and near Tiba. On the ground are wild strawberries, buttercups, and ferns. Swallows swoop, and in a clump of trees a lone mourning dove coos, a bird rarely seen or heard when Ann and Frank first visited the knoll on a clean May afternoon in 1957.

Ann continued to run the tourist farm until 2001. She donated the land to the Vermont Land Trust, which sold it to a couple who plan to keep the farm open with sheep and a large blueberry patch. It will not be run as a guest farm. Ann auctioned off the furniture and antiques in the house and now lives in a house above the property in a cleared section of the woods, not far from the knoll where she too will be buried. She will keep a couple of Scottish Highlanders. Almost every day she visits the knoll where her husband lays and the tombstone faces the view.

Lisa Kaiman — *Dairy Farmer* — Jersey Girls Dairy

There is something quirky about Lisa Kaiman's two passions — skiing and milking. She first put on skis at the age of three when her family brought her to Vermont from New Jersey to ski at Okemo ski resort, so most of us can understand the first. But *milking?* This one blossomed in 1985, when she helped out at a friend's farm in Bridport, Vermont.

"I love milking. When I'm not milking, I'm dreaming about it. It's calming. Relaxing. It gets in your blood and you can't get it out. Maybe it is the tempo of the swish, swish, swish of the milk."

This combination of sport and chore has led Lisa to create a dairy farm in Chester, Vermont, a twenty-minute drive from the ski slopes of Okemo Mountain.

Lisa planned at an early age to become a veterinarian. She graduated from the University of Vermont and decided to be a veterinarian and enrolled at another college.

"I hated vet school. It was geared toward making money. I wanted to treat only large animals, and the school poo-pooed that. Then I realized that as a

large-animal vet I would be putting down a lot of animals, because often you don't get called until it's too late. 'This is depressing,' I said. 'I'm gonna see only sick and dying animals for the rest of my life . . . That's not gonna make me happy.'"

"So I sat down and asked myself, 'When were you the happiest, when were you the most relaxed?' And it came back to milking."

Lisa returned to Vermont, where she worked a variety of jobs as she searched for a place to start a dairy. Four years later she had enough money to buy a house in Chester with 33 acres. No electricity, no running water, no kitchen, no bathrooms, no heat — but no mortgage either.

And no barn. She applied for a loan to build one, but banks don't like to give money for that; dairying is a risky venture, and the loan interest rates are

high. In Vermont the trend has been to *close* dairy farms, not start them. Lisa was told by other farmers that she was nuts to start a dairy farm; there was no way she could succeed, experts warned, particularly if she had only thirty cows, when the average Vermont farm milks one hundred and some large dairies outside of Vermont milk thousands. In addition, Lisa is not married and has no physical support beyond what is packed into her five-foot, one-inch, 100-pound body; no moral support beyond her own pluck and drive.

But perhaps this is enough. Lisa is tenacious and capable. By studying and querying other farmers, she developed a plan for an efficient, one-person farm. Then she mortgaged her house to raise the funds to build the barn and create the farm.

The barn, called a Superstructure, is shaped like a

Quonset hut but is made of woven plastic, with alternating strips of white and gray that let in light in the summer and retain heat in the winter. She designed the interior so that the cows would feed on one side and have most of the 40 x 100-foot barn for sleeping, and so she could partition the barn into sections to separate the cows when they calve.

Lisa put in a flat milking parlor so that the cows and milkers could be at the same level; one person could let the cows in and out of the parlor and also do the milking. She installed special doors with pulleys that she could open and close with one hand while sitting at a milking stool, swiveling from one cow to another. The parlor holds four cows, and the milking machines are computer controlled to automatically disengage from the udders when the cow is milked out. She installed two milk tanks; one to hold milk to be picked up by the milk truck, the other to contain colostrum and new milk to feed to newborn calves.

With the barn complete, she began her search for a herd, looking for disease-free, genetically superior stock from a clean farm with a good herd record. She wanted cows that were individually well cared for. Eventually, she settled on a herd of Jerseys (what else for a Jersey girl!), most from the farm of Danville's Sally Goodrich, who has bred Jerseys that are internationally famous, not only for their high production but also because they have beautiful lines.

Although Lisa says her love is milking, it may well be that her strongest love is where the milk comes from. She hugs her cows, talks to them in complete, intelligent sentences, gives them respect, and assures them superior lodging.

Lisa likes her cows so much she has not become certified organic. By regulation, organic farmers cannot use drugs on a cow unless they are life saving. Lisa uses aspirin, homeopathic remedies, and if the cows need antibiotics, she makes sure they get them. She also uses breeding hormones.

"If you are organic and use antibiotics, you are required to take the cow out of production for a long time. Who can afford that? I use breeding hormones because they allow me to keep a cow that otherwise I'd have to get rid of because of her failure to breed. I think the organic rules waste animals. I like my cows to be born here and to stay here as long as possible."

She uses rotational grazing, moving the cows to different sections of the pastures with the use of movable electric fences. She buys her hay. She has discovered that the only way to make a profit on a Vermont dairy farm with twenty-four milkers (she increased her herd size by four in 2002) on 25 acres of pasture is to be efficient, to be high tech, and to keep it simple.

After three years of operation, Lisa's Jerseys are paying their way, but not hers; she works from her home as a bookkeeper. She has no loans on equipment, just a mortgage on her property. Milk prices are as skittish as the commodity market, and Lisa knows she can survive ("barely") even if the price of milk goes into a bear decline. If she ever found a man that could keep up with her, and share her love of cows, she would double the size of the herd.

"My goal is for people to see that a small dairy, with a minimum amount of land and equipment, can be profitable because of the way the cows are treated — as individuals and with respect."

And what about that other passion? Twice a week during the ski season Lisa finishes up chores and drives to Okemo for a couple of hours of skiing. Each February she dries up her herd so she can take the month off and ski the Rockies. You won't find many Vermont farmers doing that.

"Cows in a stall sleep with their legs tucked under them. They're squished in there. My cows sleep in a large pen, on wood shavings. There are no stalls, and they sprawl all over the place. One morning I went in the barn and a heifer had all four legs sticking straight up in the air. 'Oh my god, she's bloated,' I said to myself. 'She's dead!' I went over and she was snoring! Yeah, my cows snore when they sleep. They sleep so well I have to wake them up.

"Most cows that I have seen on other farms live an awful life. If you let them be the calm, mellow creatures that they're supposed to be, they will be more healthy and productive. You don't have to scare or intimidate them. There is no reason for them to be nervous, excited, or jumpy. The fact is that good treatment raises production and the quality of milk."

A damp breeze sifts in from Lake Champlain and hovers over the green pastures and fields of tilled clay-soil. The moisture surrounds the barns and houses and deadens an already colorless landscape. The only sound is the honking of a flock of geese as they fly south under flat and dense clouds in a subjoined V formation. Raindrops fall spasmodically.

The Fayre Farm is just east of the town of St. Albans and 12 miles below the Canadian border, as the crow flies. The barns are old and gray, well limned, proudly capped with cupolas. Three generations of Dunsmores have increased the barn's size. Carol, the present owner, added a free-stall barn, which was caved in by a heavy snow. She rebuilt it large enough to be used for riding and training horses, but it never was.

The ceiling inside the old cow barn is low, and the side walls and posts are stained with whitewash and spiderwebs. The far end of the barn has stables for livestock; the front of the barn is jammed with dozens of carriage wheels, graceful and light, old doors, a child's rocker, bits of farm machinery, tables, horse sleighs and wagons. In a paddock adjoining the barn the cone of a plank silo squats on the ground, guarded by a belligerent ram. The silo's angled, hand-cut rafters are as carefully fitted as in a wooden tub. Strewn along the front side of the barn are fence posts wrapped in barbed wire, radiators, pumps, old pegged timber, pulley wheels, a buzz saw, a sulky, an old threshing machine, a rusted jeep ensnarled in weeds.

The house recently suffered a terrible fire, and it would appear that this farm is finished . . . but . . . the house has been rebuilt, beautiful, light, airy with

so much grace . . . go inside and see. It has an elegant spirit and you wonder . . .

The Morgans are in the pasture behind the barn, and their manes and tails are covered with burdocks. "They seem to like them," Carol says. The sheep, Border Leicesters, are penned in a pasture above a small pond and a well-shaped willow tree. They have cropped the grass skinhead bald. In the center of this pasture, on the high part, are some boulders and what look like woodchuck holes but large enough to be a fox den. Next to the pasture is a crippled wooden hay wagon; gray two by fours and two by sixes fill its bed. The farm looks like an old battlefield that has never been scavenged.

Carol's great-grandfather bought the farm in the 1890s. He was a doctor from Canada who thought it would be a healthy place for his son, who had weak lungs. Her grandfather married in 1900 and settled the farm, and Carol's father was born there in 1903. Carol bought the farm from her mother after her father died in 1971.

"It was a large dairy farm for its day," says Carol. "We had 88 milking cows and ten box stalls for young stock — about 200 head of cattle altogether, 200 sheep, 40 horses and ponies, 12 to 15 pigs, and a bunch of Border collies."

Carol increased the productivity of the herd and added Holsteins to the Ayrshires but then sold all the cows during the whole-herd buyout plan in 1987.

In 1990 Carol bought six sheep and now has one hundred ewes, one Border collie, and a handful of Morgans, including a rare gray mare she has leased out for breeding. But she admits that her cows are still supporting her.

"Unlike most farmers, I never had a love affair with machinery so I did make some money at dairy farming."

"Do you like farming?"

"What else am I going to do?"

Fayre Farm comprises 240 acres of what was once lake bottom. Most of it is rented to neighboring farms. She wants to ensure that the farm remains in the Dunsmore family, and she thinks of selling the development rights to a land trust but worries that there may be no one in her family who wants to work the land.

"Why isn't there financial incentives so that people working a small farm can make a decent living? Maybe I'll sell to a land trust and just keep the house."

Carol smiles easily. Sometimes it is a sad smile brought about by some inward thought. Other times, when she is sharing a moment with Skitter, her Border collie, it is a happy smile.

The struggle to keep this farm going could well have ended on December 17, 1999, when the frame farmhouse was badly damaged by fire.

"Well, I could have bulldozed it," Carol said. Instead she rebuilt it and redesigned the interior. The exterior looks much the same except the narrow, new clapboards are vinyl and soft yellow in color. The interior, though, is elegant and graceful. Walls have been removed to open up the downstairs so it is spacious, light, and airy. The wood floors are rich with cherry and honey maple; the walls are white. The kitchen has been remodeled and integrated with the dining room. The summer porch her grandmother added has new windows. The banister

was handmade from black walnut. Upstairs is a spare bedroom, a new Jacuzzi bathtub, an alcove office, and a Carol's small bedroom. There are books but no television.

"Why only the house?" I ask her. It is such a contrast from the barns.

"It is for my privacy," she says.

"To live here alone?"

"Oh, I have relatives who visit."

In the kitchen there is a massive side cupboard, French Canadian in style. It was charred in the fire.

"A friend of mine bought that. She died eleven years ago. We antiqued together, took fishing trips to Alaska and Baffin Island. I lost my best fishing buddy . . ." Carol is rocking silently in her chair and it squeaks as regular as a ticking clock. "Well, better get off that subject, my tears are coming already."

I think I understand. Carol's house is a jewel especially in contrast to the terminal pallor of the barns, with the decades-old detritus disintegrating in the yard. The house is an icon to one hundred years of the Dunsmores, a prominent Vermont family, and its pleasure represents the grace and beauty that she holds within her.

And just perhaps, it is also memorial to her close friend, who shared her elegance in taste, and died too soon.

Anne and Becky Burke — *Dairy Farmers* — Harvest Hill Farm

Commercial development, like a flock of grackles, has roosted within rifle shot of Harvest Hill Farm in Berlin — a sprawling, four-story hospital, several small office buildings, a large mall, and new housing. Real-estate agents with visions of breathtaking profits that could be made from the 85-acre farm pound their door. Anne Burke, who doesn't own a credit card, blows them off.

The Burkes' small farm is old fashioned. The barn is tie-stall instead of free-stall and Ayrshire cows, rather than heavy-production Holsteins, file to and from the pasture during the summer. Behind the barn is a manure pile. It has the sweet, sour smell of nutrient-rich manure, pasture processed, and not the acrid and rank soup found in the manure pits near large free-stall barns. The sugarhouse is slightly larger than a corncrib, some of the tractors date back to the 1940s, and it takes three people to move the small hay bales into the dark end of the hayloft. In the spring the driveway is as muddy as the manure pile after a downpour. There is no dishwashing machine in the kitchen; in fact, the sink, stained and grimy, goes back to the day the Burkes moved into this farm on August 10, 1963.

You can't make a profit with a small farm, says the Vermont Agriculture Department, extension agents, and the farmers who are moving up to larger herds, manure pits, and tractors. No way.

Anne Burke just laughs. "I'm against the world." She is a facsimile of one of the dried-apple dolls they sell in folk craft stores. Her face is crinkled and wrinkled, her smile wide, her gray hair tautly pulled back. An old T-shirt covers her short stature. There's nothing shy about Anne, whose accent is as Yankee-rich as a can of B grade maple syrup, and in that head of hers whirls some wheels as sharp as a new cutter bar.

The Burke's farm is all family. Anne runs it. Her husband, Ray, whom she met on the dance floor of the Tunbridge World's Fair, is blind. He recently retired as dispatcher for the Vermont Highway Department. Every Vermonter knows his voice, as he reported, sometimes for thirty hours straight, the conditions of Vermont roads during floods and blizzards. Now he grumbles happily that he is working harder than ever with the farm chores. Their son Kelly and his wife, Renée, work full time on the farm. Helping out at certain times of the year are

and her herd shows it; she recently sold one at auction for $4,000, "and that buyer was mighty tickled." She also sells milkers, show cows and calves to 4-H'ers. She rents cows as stand-ins at political rallies, for educational purposes at school, or for cow shit bingo. (Tape squares on the grass, sell the squares and set the cow loose. Whoever holds the number of the square where the cow plops, why it's Cow Shit Bingo!)

When the manure pile gets high, Anne will say to Kelly, "We got money in the bank." Anne is not concerned about the development that surrounds her farm. "They make good customers." Kelly will load a pickup full of fresh manure and deliver it to people who want it for their gardens — at $50 a load. The wreaths and garlands the family makes at Christmas puts $15,000 into their pockets. They sell pumpkins and squash in the fall and once turned the profits into new boots for the family. She sells farm-fresh eggs and maple syrup that she finishes off on her kitchen stove and cans herself. Then there are her elkhounds. "The puppies we sold paid for the last 8 acres of land we bought." Oh yes, and every other day the Agri-Mark milk truck sucks up 2,500 gallons of Ayrshire milk from their cooler.

Anne is also a water witch — she is very adept at finding wells with a forked apple stick. A large well-drilling company hires her to dowse before they drill, and she almost always finds water. She often takes along granddaughter Becky, who is learning the art. "When we're out dowsing — and they pay mighty well — I say to Becky, 'We're paying for your college education one well at a time.' I dowse deep veins. Some well drillers have gone to 1,000 feet without dowsing, but if they called me first they would probably go down only 300. I dowsed for one guy who went down 180 feet and got 30 gallons a minute . . . I know a couple of spots in Vermont I call the Sahara Desert and . . . how did I learn? I dunno. My father couldn't lick a stone with his feet

Lynn, Vera, Shelly, Tammy, Rose, Lucia, and Sam — daughters, granddaughters, sons, and in-laws. Just about everyone pitches in when they are making wreaths and garlands that decorate the streets of Montpelier and Northfield during the Christmas season.

Most important to Anne is their eighteen-year-old granddaughter, Becky. Pretty and self-assured, she is beginning her first year at agricultural school in Randolph. "She's a real Vermont farm girl," says Anne. "Whatever she does she is going to do it right, and I appreciate that. When she's through with school I'll be training her to run this farm. You know . . . each one of our kids grew up raising a heifer. That was their first bank account." Harvest Hill Farm is a mini-conglomerate with a number of subsidiaries,

although Anne wouldn't put it quite that way.

"Careful management, that's how we do it," says Anne. "We manage like no one else does, and we do all the chores ourselves. That's the Vermont way.

"Take our Ayrshires. Pretty, huh? Well if they're good enough for a Scotch man, they're good enough for me. They're a long-life cow, with a good tight udder, and we've got cows we've been milking for ten years . . . those new big farms can go through a milker in eighteen months!

"Now a cow of ours has to be one of two things. She's got to be one heck of a show cow or she's got to be one heck of a milk cow, and if she isn't . . . well, bye-bye."

Anne reads up on genetics while others are watching television. She selects her bulls carefully

in the water, but my grandfather could. When he dowsed I went with him. I cut an apple stick and tried it and said, 'Look, Grandpa, I can do it too.' Either you do it or you don't."

If anything makes this farm tick, it is Anne's shrewdness and salesmanship and her penchant to use and maintain old equipment.

"Take those new big farms with four hundred or more cows. They got overhead like there is no tomorrow. They like 150 horsepower tractors, and I'm glad to stick to my old Massey and the McCormick from the1930s and that old Cub. They just keep a-ticking.

"They got lots of hired help, and they better have a good manager to keep the herd up to date and healthy. They go through a cow in one and a half lactations and they don't even breed her back. That's why we sell every heifer we have. They're nothing but factory farms. They got so much manure there's no place to put it, so it goes in those large storage pits. All the nutrients leach out, and what's left stinks and is good for nothing.

"The small farms will be here long after those big ones are gonzo. Small farms are family farms, and there is always someone coming along to do what you are doing.

"A lot of farming is anticipation of what's coming. You go to work in an office and you know it is going to be the same thing today as what it is tomorrow. You don't when you are farming. You take it as it comes. There are good days and there are bad days. When the hay is all raked up and I roll into the field with the baler and down pours the rain, well you make the best of what you can't help, but there's this satisfaction of helping birth the new calf, to see the garden grow and the squash that you will sell turn yellow. It's the anticipation of what's coming. That's farming. You take it as it comes."

Carrie Chalmers — *Gardener* — QUOYBURRAY FARM

Carrie Chalmers was twenty-four when she appeared in the book *Vermont People*. She was a Brown University graduate who turned her back on the job recruiters to return to the small family farm in Weston in order to garden. At that time she mentioned that because of high land prices she could never establish a commercial garden, so she used 2 acres of her parents' 19-acre farm.

In her first year of gardening, in 1989, she made $260 from vegetable and fruit sales. Then she left for four years to apprentice on a garden in Martha's Vineyard. In 1995 she returned home to open Quoyburray Farm, named for an ancestral farm in the Orkney Islands in Scotland.

Carrie is now thirty-four, married for a year and a half, and expecting her first child in the summer of 2002. She looks much as she did in 1989, smoothly beautiful with a thick mass of red hair lightly burnished by the summer sun. She is thinner but sinewy; hoeing can do that. Carrie loves hoeing. She would rather hoe all day than talk to people. These days, though, as her belly grows, she is reflecting on her past years as a gardener, and her future, as a gardener and a mother.

"I grew up with the idea that you feed the soil. My dad taught me that. We always had animals and manure, and we never used pesticides or herbicides. I loved the idea of aiding plants to grow in the short and harsh growing season we have here, and of observing them closely."

As she expanded her vegetable and flower gardens, Carrie had the freedom of no mortgage payments, because the land belonged to her parents. The other costs, though, were, to the young gardener, "an ungodly amount of money." The first greenhouse cost $8,000, and then, in a year of drought, she had an artesian well drilled that saved the crop, but cost another $8,000. She built another greenhouse for $8,000, and bought a small tractor, and two tomato tunnels at $1,000 each, and then, well . . . she ended up with loans and high interest payments.

2000 was a summer of rain. A cloud burst dumped 8 inches of rain in a few square miles. Roads were gutted and runoff waters almost obliterated her garden.

Over time Carrie's reputation grew — she became an expert on uncommon annuals, and she quickly sold her vegetables and flowers at the local farmers' market.

More and more often she was asked if she was certified.

"No," she would answer, ". . . but I don't use herbicides, I don't use pesticides, I don't use treated seeds or synthetic fertilizer."

Then a restaurant owner asked to put her name on the menu and say she was an organic grower, but because she wasn't certified they couldn't use the word *organic*.

"What is certified?" she asks. "It is a high expense. I know that. There are big California farmers who buy tons of organic fertilizers and pesticides and ship their organic produce across the country. Who would you rather support, a local farmer that you know and trust or a massive organic farm from California? The government supports the bigger industry. They give subsidies to them. We small farmers don't count. It's a very hard choice — whether to be so small that you work yourself to death trying to pay your bills or become so big that you lose control of what you grow and to whom you sell."

But it's the weather that most rankles Carrie. Weston is in a mountainous microclimate best suited for growing potatoes. The old-time farmers knew that.

"The climate stinks, the soil stinks, and there are rocks everywhere. It is either too wet or too dry. The growing season is early June to early September, and even then it is chilly and retards growth. The mountains hide the sun in the morning and evening. The growing season is maybe two weeks longer only 30 miles from here . . ."

Carrie pauses and looks inward, thinking about her plants. "Lettuce does great, though . . . and the tomatoes grow well in their tunnels . . . but it is so frustrating. Growing vegetables and flowers overlapped, and I just couldn't handle the work and couldn't afford to hire people at what they should be paid."

Starting in the summer of 2002 and thinking as a mother and gardener, Carrie plans to grow vegetables only for her family and friends. She will focus on flowers, and the first step is to design a large perennial garden in front of her greenhouses.

"It will be a beautiful garden with perennials and herbs mixed together. I will plant apple trees and blueberry bushes and have display beds. The vegetable garden will be separate but well designed so it

is also beautiful. People will come to see how flowers are used and learn from the combination of colors and textures.

"Flowers have a potential for a better return with less labor. It's just me in the garden, and I don't want to be overworked, particularly in the first year of my baby's life."

There's also the possibility she will supplement her income by working with her brother, who owns a small property-maintenance business. Nurseries and landscaping work very well together, and she has taken garden-design courses. Carrie would design and plant gardens for the many summer residents and could eventually hire a gardening crew. She is also writing more articles about gardening.

"Whatever happens," Carrie says, "I will always be in the dirt. I will always be working with plants."

Colleen Goodridge — *Sawmill* — Goodridge Lumber

The Goodridge lumberyard, just south of the town of Albany in the Northeast Kingdom, is carved into a hillside that once sloped down to a brook. It is a typical lumberyard: towering stacks of logs with their butts chalk-marked surround the open stall sawmill. The yard is a gruel of mud, bark, and sawdust churned together by the trucks and loaders. The medium-pitched hum of the diesel engines, the whine of the chipper, and the brief, chalkboard screech of the band saw are the music of a busy day. Like most sawmills, this one is a soggy place — except on those dry summer days when the wind is fresh and cool and freshly cut lumber scents the yard.

But on this damp October day it's another scent I smell mixed in with the diesel fumes of the loader and wafting between the log piles and the sawmill. It is perfume. *Good perfume.* Where in hell does that come from?

Colleen Goodridge is driving the loader. She stops next to a load of logs just brought in, hops out, hard hat on, and tallies the board feet. She is the scented one and flashes me a quick smile under her hard hat. There is an intimacy in the way she greets strangers.

The Goodridge Lumber Company is a family business. Colleen is the boss; she answers the phones, does the paperwork, deals with the suppliers, oversees the direction of the company. Her three sons work with her. Doug is the sawyer and makes the mill scream and sets the pace of the day's production. Mark is the planer. Brian works in the yard loading and unloading both logs and cut lumber.

Colleen grew up in a neighboring town on a small dairy farm with registered Jerseys. She, her three sisters, and her brother all had chores. They milked,

helped with haying, and worked in the sugarbush tapping maple trees and gathering sap. They were 4-H members and showed their cattle at local fairs.

"I think this early background is what made me what I am," says Colleen. "We developed an appreciation of growing things, and we learned to help younger people."

Colleen married and lived with her husband, Donly, in a trailer on 2 acres where the mill was eventually built. They thought how wonderful it would be to build a log home, which they achieved in 1974. Then they thought it would be fun to sell their own logs so they bought an old sawmill for $500 and powered it with a tractor.

By 1983 they had a full mill turning white cedar — the local tree — into logs for cabins.

But in 1992 there was a "change in the family structure" as Colleen puts it. The result was that she and her husband separated; he got the logging business and lumber lots. She was left with the sawmill. Her sons decided that they wanted to work with her.

Today, one hundred loggers from a 60-mile radius supply enough white cedar to saw 1.2 million feet per year, or enough for about sixty-five log cabins. White cedar, found in swampland, is slow-growing, rot-resistant, and has extremely good insulating properties because of the amount of airspace within the wood.

In the spring the Goodridge family holds seminars for carpenters and homeowners on cabin construction, materials, caulking, joining, and maintenance.

"We find more people want to live closer to the land," Colleen says, "and I think you feel that spirit when you live in a log home."

Colleen enjoys the competitiveness of running a

business that feeds six families (besides the Goodridges there are two employees), and she likes its roughness.

"We're not afraid to get dirty. I can be out there fixing the motor covered with grease, or I can be in the mud scaling logs. But I was also chairman for the local school board for seven years, and we developed a plan for a new school. When I was due to attend a meeting with the Education Department, I cleaned up, fixed my hair, put on high heels, and I was not a sawmill worker but Chairman of the School Board introducing the Vermont Commissioner of Education to the people of Albany.

"What I like is the combination of working with my family and being connected to the land. You smell it and you feel it. Every day is different on the ridge. We can watch the first green leaf bloom and the deer drink in the stream. Sometimes a moose wanders through our yard. It's a feeling that goes back to my days on the farm when we all worked together and did our jobs and felt good about what we did. Now we're not on the farm milking or haying, but we are close to the land and its natural resources.

"It is a privilege to work with my three sons. I am pleased that they, in this world of take-take-take, go beyond what a lot of young men do. Two of the boys are in the volunteer fire department. Mark is a member of the planesman association and attends annual meetings in Maine. I was the first woman director of the Vermont Forest Products Association, and I am a trustee of the Methodist Church. We give back to the community."

The name of the perfume she wears, along with a yellow hard hat and steel-toe boots, is Ici.

Janet Bailey — *Sustainable Farmer* — Fair Winds Farm

Janet Bailey and her family live on Fair Winds Farm in Brattleboro. They named it that because fair winds brought them there. She is articulate about the life she and her family follow — sustainable farming.

"We had just started a family and were thrashing around, trying to find our direction. At the time we were working as farmers and gardeners at a camp in Plymouth. We decided to buy land for ourselves when we heard that a small land trust in Brattleboro was looking for people to take over a piece of property and do some farming.

"Claude Tate owned the farm. He was eighty years old and had been on it for seventy-five years. He lived alone, and he no longer had animals. He heard about the land trust and called them up. 'See if you can find somebody to farm here and take care of me, as I don't want to leave this place until I die. They can have use of the house, and I stay in part of it.'

"We came to visit him and brought our two small girls. It was the kind of cluttered farmhouse where there were paths between piles of old newspapers and magazines. One led to the stove, another to the sink, and one to the bedroom. That was it. The kerosene smell just about knocked me over.

"Jay and I looked at each other. 'I dunno,' I said. We told Claude we would see what we could do. I guess he liked us because he called up as soon as we got home, wanting to know when we would move in.

"So we moved down with one Jersey and some pigs and chickens and he seemed so happy and excited. We started to clean up the house, but left two weeks later to get more of our stuff. When we returned there was a note on the door: Claude had had a heart attack and was in the hospital. Six weeks later I had my baby, and Claude moved back home. So I was caring for two daughters, a husband, a sick old man, and my premature baby. The first years were kind of thin and it was hand-to-mouth. We had no capital, but we had milk, meat, eggs, and produce. We heated the house by wood we cut, but it was always freezing because there was no insulation. We just maintained the property until we formed an idea of what we were doing here. This was in 1978. Claude died in 1980.

"We decided to grow vegetables and sell the produce locally. The farmers' market in Brattleboro was very small and dying and needed growers. We joined the board and helped them get organized. On our first day at the market we set up a card table and sold a bushel of spinach. There were only ten vendors — it was hippies back then — but it grew. The Brattleboro Farmers' Market once grossed $10,000 a year but now does $12–13,000 each Saturday.

"I worked as a part–time nurse four nights a week. I was mother, cook, egg collector, and I did the planting and growing. Jay's expertise was cultivating and caring for the land, and his passion was — and is — Suffolk Punch workhorses. We now have 5 workhorses, 325 chickens, and 5 pigs.

"This is a horse-powered, organic, sustainable, diversified family farm of 42 acres. I shouldn't use the word *organic*; we are not certified. Certification is needed for large growers whose buyers do not have contact with them. Our customers know us and our farm, and we tell them what our practices are. Now I see certified organic produce that comes labeled with a big plastic tag — it's so blatant. What is an organic farmer doing with plastic labels? It has nothing to do with sustainability. The big guys are getting into it because they see money in the word *organic*.

"Diversification is the key. We try to balance our income among eggs, vegetables, flowers, and horses, which includes sleigh rides and horse workshops, so if there's a drought, or no snow, one of our other endeavors will cover the bill.

"Each enterprise we have uses resources from the others. The pigs eat garden waste; the chickens eat grain and fresh stuff from the garden. Their manure goes back on the garden and fields. The horses tie into everything. We use them to haul logs, till the land, mow the hay. We found that a tractor compacts the land too much.

"We picked this lifestyle for ourselves and our children. We wanted to bring our kids up on the land. They watched and helped us with our chores. Because kids' work is to play, we did not give them chores before school. They are grown now. Erica, our eldest, lives in a cabin on our farm. She graduated from Haverford College in Pennsylvania as an English major and decided she wanted to come home to give back to her community, so she teaches in our school system. Her college friends couldn't believe she wanted to come home, and when they first met her they didn't believe she grew up on a farm. It is prejudice and our kids grew up with that, but they had a real life on which to center their lives.

"We have weekend seminars to teach people to use draft horses. Just after September 11 we had our Suffolk Punch weekend. It was such an awful time and we didn't think anyone would come, but it was a large crowd. They said it was so wonderful to have something real to do that weekend.

"One of the reasons our workshops are growing is that so many people have global concerns. We've been doing workshops for six years; and in the past two years more people want to buy a farm or get away from their high-powered job. They seem to hate what they're doing.

"In the past there was a lot of innocence in the back-to-the-land movement but the word is out that it's not easy, so people are studying and planning carefully. They come here to learn how to handle a horse in a barn, how to harness it, hitch it to wagons and plows and cultivators. At mealtime we talk about gardening and raising animals and other things from A to Z. Many of them are already on this path with wood heat and gardens. There's a quiet undercurrent going on in Vermont and elsewhere that is different from building big houses on hills, and if you're in it, then you're aware of what's going on and the number of people swimming down to our level.

"I feel horsepower makes senses. It makes us independent from gas and oil, which are at the roots of our conflicts. People are concerned about atmosphere, global warming, and being independent. When electricity and gas goes, what happens? We have solar hot water and are trying to reduce our reliance on outside input for monetary, environmental, and social reasons. We feel strongly that the roots of violence and wars has to do with our oil policy.

"Sustainability — living the way we do — is a social and spiritual belief. If we believe in peace, then we have to stop causing violence. The fighting is not over horses and food but money and power. A lot of young people are very concerned about this. So are we."

The Bartholomew Sisters — *Dairy Farmers* — BARTHOLOMEW BROTHERS FARM

In the late 1920s, two sisters, Florence and Louise Munger, married two brothers, Clyde and Hollis Bartholmew, who were farming in Benson, Vermont. Half a century later two sisters, Clare and Jeanne Moriarty, married Donald and Peter, two sons of the Munger-Bartholomew unions. These four brothers-sisters-wives-husbands, along with another brother and his wife, run the Bartholomew farm started so long ago.

Their farm, a gathering of weather-stressed barns and frame houses, stretches for 5 miles on West Road. There are two neatly trimmed ranch houses, homes for the original sister-widows, Florence and Louise, whose husbands are buried in the family cemetery a short distance from their homes. A scat-tering of abandoned cars and farm machinery supply used parts. Corn and hay fields slope down from the woods, and there are more deer than you could ever count. The Bartholmews are an old breed of Vermonters who believe in two adages: *If you can't fix it you shouldn't be farming,* and *Farmers don't want to own all the land, just those pieces that hitch onto their farm.* In 1928 the Bartholomew farm included 200 acres; now it is 4,000 acres.

Clare Bartholmew and her husband, Donald, raised their four sons in the old farmhouse on the hill overlooking the main farm and field. When they moved in, during the fall of 1980, the chimney had fallen in, leaving a big hole in the center of the house, and coons lived upstairs. After their second son was born, they renovated the upstairs, and the coons retreated to a back room; but, with rabies spreading into Vermont and more children on the way, the coons lost out to Spud, their coon-killing dog, and a .22 rifle. Today, the 200-year-old house looks worn down. The porch is sagging from the weight of boxes stuffed with the detritus of farming. A rifle with no stock leans just inside the front porch. The living room is comfortable and looks like a trophy room for 4-H awards. Siding is missing on the old barn, and bales of hay peep out between the barn's skeleton — 8 x 8 hand-cut beams. Clare's goats occupy the bottom of the barn; the cows are kept in the free-stall barn a mile away. A cornfield acts as a fence to the lawn.

Clare has that take-charge personality you expect to find in a master sergeant, a quality she has honed over the past twenty years as she raised her four boys, tended her goats and a big garden, did the housework, cooked, shopped, toted the kids, and most of all, helped her four children become deeply involved in 4-H, an education program run by cooperative extension services and the Agriculture Department.

"The purpose of 4-H is to make the best better, that is the motto," says Clare. "Caring and owning animals teaches them responsibility. They have to keep a record book on their animal, how much and what they feed it, the costs, how much it grows. They learn how to prepare them and show their animals at county fairs. They do oral presentations to their peers, give talks to children at fairs, and attend 4-H functions and fairs in other states.

"You know there are kids in our local school who don't know a thing about animals — what a cow eats or drinks, or that you have to milk them twice a day and they have four teats. And no, chocolate milk does not come from brown cows."

The 4-H program, and living on a family farm, has directed the young Bartholomews' careers. David has an associate degree in dairy management from Vermont Technical College and is on the dean's list at the University of Vermont, where he is in the Animal Science Program. Sam is in college majoring in animal science and biochemistry and plans to be a veterinarian or a teacher. Charles's interests have been baseball and football, but he just entered Vermont Technical College. Justin, the youngest and very active in 4-H, is a sophomore in high school.

"We farm, we hunt, we fish," says Clare, "when we aren't farming or preparing animals for the country fairs." Ice fishing is their favorite winter occupation, and deer hunting becomes a family affair as dozens of Bartholomews arrive to hunt the 4,000 acres of land. "It's a family toot," says Clare.

Clare has a degree in physical education and never forgot that her training is as a teacher. Now, at the age of forty-five, after raising her four sons, she has finished a course in special education and will teach at the Fair Haven high school full time as a teacher's aid.

"I wouldn't do it when the kids were growing. We probably could have fixed things up around here if I was out working, but staying at home with kids is important and you don't know what you are missing until you have done it. I am a big pusher for people staying home with their kids. I see the need for it. I see kids who don't have a sense of belonging because their parents are working or divorced and they ship their kids to day care. I'm not saying day care is not a good thing for some people in some instances but I think, why have a kid if you are not going to stay home with them?"

Her sister Jeanne Bartholomew lives down the road, in another classic farmhouse next to an old, tired-looking barn, stark as a scene from *Ethan Frome*. She has an easy smile and is more introspective about farming.

"I came here as a milkmaid and worked for four years and then married my boss, Peter," Jeanne says between chores. "That was in 1978, so Peter and I have been farming for quite a few years. Now I take care of the calves morning and evening." Jeanne has a degree in animal science from the University of Vermont, while Peter milks and does much of the

or pasture. If this farmer goes out of business, these neighbors get nervous because they think houses will replace the cows in their view, so they want to limit the farmers to protect their property. That kind of thinking is weaseling its way into Vermont, and I feel strongly about it. People who move here enjoy our way of life, but quite often they want to change things right off. They have to have garbage removal and sidewalks and paved roads and zoning. Someone will have to pay for it, and I am not too much for that kind of change. I like to keep things back here on the farm the way they are.

"I was single when I moved to Benson and I bought land when I was nineteen, but I needed a well and pump to water the horses, so I had to have electricity. And then I lived in a trailer, and I got electricity and a phone, and once you have these services, it's hard to live without them.

"I dream of ice fishing in Alaska or a place a little more removed from here. I thought we would live and die here, but there is encroachment coming in and . . ."

"You got 4,000 acres, you are surrounded by fields and woods and animals, and you feel encroachment?" I say. Jeanne laughs.

"I always pictured myself to be self-sufficient and not have power and the phone and that kind of thing. I would like to go back to that."

vet work. Clare's husband, Donald, and Neal do the field work; Don also runs the family sawmill. They milk 142 cows, a mix of Holsteins and Ayrshires.

"We're a very self-sufficient group of farmers. We build our houses from trees from our property and turned into lumber in our own sawmill. We do the plumbing and wiring. Donny can fix anything. We have outside wood furnaces that heat our houses and water and we only burn wood from our land. We have no hired hands, just our kids and us." Jeanne also has had a real-estate license for the past twenty years and sells real estate part time. It has made her sensitive to the value of land use.

"We would never sell our development rights to the Vermont Land Trust or Nature Conservancy. Our investment is in our property's resale value if

someone chooses not to farm in the future. It's a good chance that this farm will stay in business, but I don't want it predetermined by someone else who will say this is what you can or cannot do, twenty or thirty years down the road. I think farmers who are in financial distress will sell development rights to keep the farm going, but the money they get doesn't go far. I'm against it.

"I differ with a lot of groups that say land belongs to everybody and you have to protect it. I know that farmers are conscientious about their property and have their life savings invested in the land. They don't want to see it destroyed or polluted, but they also don't want to see someone come in and tell them what to do. As a real-estate agent I sell land or homes that is sometimes next to a farmer's hay field

Kate Hodges — *Apple Grower* — Sunrise Orchards

What do you do when you're an actor living in New York City and your growing family puts you on the financial edge? Do you go back to your roots or stick it out? Barney and Dee Hodges opted for roots, but instead of returning to Barney's family farm in Virginia, they moved their young children to a scrabbled hillside near Middlebury to scratch out an apple orchard, which they named Sunrise Orchards.

At the age of six, Kate Hodges was doing chores in the new apple orchard. At nine she learned to drive the tractor. As a teenager — alongside her father, mother, brother, and sister — Kate was planting new trees, thinning older ones, applying fertilizer, and in the fall picking apples, sorting them for quality, size, and color, and then hauling them by tractor to the barn.

The Macs, Paula Reds, and Empires that they grew earned a reputation for quality, but the copious harvest from the 160 acres of trees they planted was more than the family could handle, and local help was hard to find. In 1978 they signed on to a program that brought Jamaican workers to Vermont during apple season. Fifteen of them were the first to work on Sunrise Orchards, and young Kate became their friend.

"It was a cultural change, and they opened up the orchard to another world. It was exciting for all of us," Kate says. "I got to know them real well."

Picking apples is a fussy job. Top-quality apples are hand picked at the moment when the size is big and the color glows. They have to be handled very gently so they don't bruise, and there can be no bad apples in the bin. The Jamaicans are quick but

gentle, and it is one reason why the Sunrise Orchards apples are the pick of the crop. Kate's job during the harvest is to work with the Jamaicans and to check the quality of apples that are picked. "I'm sort of a cheerleader," she says.

The Jamaicans live on the property in bunkhouses. The Hodges turned a barn into a dining room, which has one wall decorated with a huge mural Kate drew. Then she hand-painted T-shirts for her friends.

Kate has been drawing longer than she has been driving a tractor, and the urge for art grew stronger as she matured. She worked part time on the farm and as an art teacher. It was overload.

"I was teaching seventy-five to one hundred kids a day, and it was like a factory," she says. "I never worked my own art. So I quit and decided to go somewhere to reflect. I went to Alaska, and on the summer solstice of 1999 I spent six days on a glacier. I drew a lot and wrote in my journal. And I thought, here I am in this stark place, when I go back to my life, what do I want to accomplish? What do I really want to do? And I realized the land I grew up on is so

incredibly special — I want to spend time there and get to know my family as an adult. I want to return to that environment and work on the farm and my art."

Kate returned, and in a woodlot surrounded by rows of apple trees humming in the springtime from thousands of rented pollinating bees, she erected a 30-foot diameter yurt. Originally designed by nomads in Mongolia, this yurt was made in Oregon and has a Plexiglas skylight in the center of the roof, windows, and is covered with insulated and laminated waterproof fabric. Kate moved in and adapted to a rather minimalist life. She transports jugs of water from the barn, uses kerosene lamps (there is no electricity), and cooks on a camp stove fueled by propane that also cools her refrigerator. In the winter she heats with wood, although the yurt turns frigid in the morning and the trip to the self-composting outhouse is an eye opener.

Kate has set up a large table in the yurt where she works on her art — painting, creating sculpture with burdocks, thorns, milkweed, lichen, and other items she finds in the woods. Most recently she created a hand-crafted book of her latest art — tree painting. It isn't unusual to see Kate 40 feet in the air in a mountaineer harness, bracing herself against a beech tree, and applying brush strokes to the trunk.

"I was looking at the beech trees, and I noticed that they were very long, smooth surfaces and that the limbs and the trunks looked like body parts, so I started drawing these arms and hands and faces at the base and just worked my way up. I get into this meditative state drawing on the trees."

"Kate — she's crazy," says Grassy, one of her closest Jamaican friends, who has been coming to the orchard for twenty-four years and is one of twenty-five Jamaicans now working on the farm. Then he laughs.

Kate smiles. "They respect me for what I am doing and know that art is as much part of my life as the orchard. It's a healthy way to live."

Debbie Hazelton — *Sawyer* — Hell's Peak Farm

Halfway through the 20th century the small towns of Weston, Peru, Landgrove, Londonderry, and Winhall were poorly populated towns of woods, pastures, fields, and gravel roads. During April — Mud Season — cars bogged down in middle of the roads on the way to Manchester or Rutland, the nearest big towns. A smattering of summer people were sprinkled about and a few ski lodges surrounded Big Bromley ski resort. Weston had a summer theater, but most locals made a meager living, logging, working in sawmills, or farming. Workhorses were used to skid out freshly cut logs, gather maple sap, and mow the hay fields, although the Ford tractor was quickly replacing them. People bartered for their necessities, and it seemed that every other town had a *nimrod* — a local woodsman who poached deer and sold the meat to the locals. There were no lawn and garden crews and few caretakers; the town plow cleared driveways. Junk cars were the outdoor sculpture of choice. At this time the price on 200 acres of a broke-back farm with a porcupine-gnawed barn was under $10,000.

In the 1960s Stratton and then Magic Mountain ski resorts were carved onto the mountains. The road over the mountain from Weston to Ludlow was paved and opened year-round. The interstate highway system reached north toward Canada. Farmers' land was parceled up and sold. Tyrolean-style "cookie-cutter houses" came into style and were quickly followed by the waste-of-space A-frame. Condominiums entered the local lexicon, and real-estate offices spread like weeds in a garden. Town trucks no longer plowed driveways or helped tow cars out of the ditch, for the cost was

high and any perceived damage could lead to a lawsuit.

Expensively remodeled farmhouses and new faux-country homes appeared in the 1970s and 1980s. By the 1990s the region was becoming gentrified, and the new trend was toward oversized tract mansions built ostentatiously on hillsides. Historic, rambling stone walls were pilfered or torn down and rebuilt to reflect the wealthy order of these new, often absent, residents. Chemicals were added to designer ponds to change their color from algae green to blue. Farmers' hay fields, if they didn't become estates, grew back into woods and real-estate developers smiled, for they could fit more houses into woods and still retain the feeling of privacy.

Stratton Mountain, once the habitat of bears, is now a multimillion dollar ski and summer resort. Peru, Landgrove, and Weston are homes to many people who are considerably more than well-to-do. Young natives will be very lucky to ever afford a piece of land. Two hundred acres of land and a broken-down farm would now cost a half-million dollars, and a not-so-hot building lot can sell for $25,000.

On the other hand, many of the sons and daughters who did not leave Vermont now have service jobs that give them a higher income then their parents. There is a local medical clinic that offers friendly and effective service, there is an efficient local rescue squad, and the local school, Flood Brook, is praised for its high standard of education. And many of the gravel roads have been paved, which is not necessarily an improvement; Landgrove, a town clustered with expensive homes,

tries to keep some feeling of integrity with their past by not allowing any of their roads to be paved.

Debbie and Donald Hazelton have lived with much of this change. Their home is just off a back road between Londonderry and Landgrove, on property Donald's father owned. Debbie was a school-teacher who wanted to work outside, so she quit her job and worked with her husband, who logged and cut firewood. For twenty years, starting in the late 1970s, they operated a small sawmill across from Donald's mother's house. At the time, these small family-run lumber mills provided much of the board feet that locals needed to build a house, barn, or garage, and often the lumber was cut to specification and the price was low. Chances were that the buyer and the sawyer were neighborly and used to trading with each other.

Debbie and Don went through three sawmills. The first one burned, the second wore out, and then they bought a steel mill, which was designed to stay in one place. Debbie often ran it while her husband logged. It was hard work for one person. Debbie peaveyed the logs onto the track and sawed them.

She removed the tailings from the carriage and threw them in one pile and then stacked the lumber she had sawn. Then she walked back to the big saw and cut some more. Debbie had a knack for sawing a log into halves and quarters.

Over time, the new Vermonters — particularly the second-home owners — needed somebody to cut their lawns, shape up their gardens, and clean the woods. And so the Hazeltons adapted to the new economy — today Debbie mows lawns and at other times works with her husband in the woods. She has also developed her avocation, homeopathy, and now has an office in nearby Manchester.

But the cultural change affected the Hazeltons' income from the sawmill. The locals who bought lumber from them were cutting costs when they built anything, and the new residents went to the big lumberyard in Manchester to buy lumber, sometimes milled in Canada or the West. Their business fell away and the few remaining customers were not enough to pay their costs.

The mill had become a burden. In 1998 the Hazeltons shut down their lumber mill. They intend to move it next to their house and use it to produce their own lumber. Don is logging, sometimes on land bought at a high price by an out-of-stater, and will prune the woods, open up a view, prep a home site, and log or clear the rest of the woods. Debbie is now mowing thirty lawns with the help of her two daughters. She's forgotten where she stored the peavey.

Barbara Carpenter — *Dairy Farmer* — CARPENTER FARM

It is ironic that the small-farm movement, in contrast to the large dairy and chicken operations now expanding in Vermont and across the nation, takes its model from the farms that operated in Vermont fifty years ago. That model could just as well be Carpenter Farm.

The farm, dead ended on a steep dirt road west of Cabot, was built, as most old farms were, into the lee side of a mountain. The design and placement of the fields, house, and barn is minimalist; it is the type of operation that supports one family and can be worked by a team of horses. The house faces south-southwest, so it gathers what little warmth and light there is in the winter sun. It is a plank house, built in 1830 of hand-hewn timbers and 3-inch-thick boards cut by a water-driven, up-and-down saw. The barn is wedged into a hill and has sixteen stalls designed for the smaller stature of the Jersey cow. Above the stalls is tractor and wagon storage, and above that is the hayloft. A forest of hard- and soft-wood encircle the farm, and 30 acres of pastures and fields surround the house. The maple sugarbush is a five-minute walk from the front door. This farm was horse-powered before the horses were replaced by a 1951 International and a younger, more powerful John Deere tractor.

The farm goes back to a time when most everything was fixed and made by the farmer or his neighbors. Take the water line, for instance. It runs a quarter mile from the spring to the barn, and the pipe is augered through 12-foot sections of fir trees, called pump logs, laid end to end and then buried. It feeds into a wooden tub planted in the barnyard. The tub was made in nearby East Corinth by Maurice Page. The auger that cut the hole through the fir logs hangs in the barn.

Barbara Blachy is a keen-eyed woman, small but stern in purpose and strength, who bought this farm in 1947 when she was eighteen. Born in New Jersey, the daughter of a food and vegetable broker, she lived on West 4th Street in New York City when she visited a friend in Vermont. She paid $100 for a house in bad shape but with a good spine and 8 acres of land. The property taxes were $12 a year.

"The farm was totally run down. It was completely

unproductive, not farmed for years, and the house was in terrible shape, and I had to build a barn. Even so, I thought I was Queen of the World."

In 1953 Barbara moved in and spent the summer evenings sleeping in a hammock slung between two apple trees as she reconstructed the house. With some family financing she built a barn and added a few acres and bought a Jersey heifer. Within a few years, she had worked the fields into shape and increased the herd to three milkers.

Of course she met the neighbors. Charles Carpenter was the son of the farmer whose patched fields and barn placemarked a hillside a couple of miles distant, and he offered to help out. Barbara now had seven cows to milk.

In 1959 Barbara and Charles were married. He liked her philosophy on farming, which is to keep it small and compact. The farm has never supported more than twelve milkers.

And work they did. They planted apple trees and Christmas trees and a large garden. Horses, ponies, sheep, chickens, and ducks joined the Jerseys. They slowly added parcels of land to their farm, sometimes paying no more than $15 an acre.

The horses twitched out the cut logs, sledged maple sap to the sugarhouse, and in the winter a horse-drawn pung brought the milk down the snow-covered road to the transfer station. During the summer they loaded daily the four polished milk cans, 80 pounds when full, on the back of their pickup and drove them 3½ miles to the Cabot Creamery.

All the wood they cut was with a crosscut saw and an ax.

"I never did use a chain saw. We used a crosscut to saw all our sugar wood and split it into 4-foot lengths — I can't believe we did that. Cut and split by hand our house wood too. An old-timer showed me how to use a broad ax to build my first barn. I just loved working in the woods and driving wagons."

In 1981 Charles died, and, well, you don't miss a day's milking do you? Her days grew long. Barbara rose before dawn and milked the cows. During hay season she hitched the horses and mowed the fields from 6:00 A.M. to dark, then did the evening milking, and finished up an hour before midnight. She needed help, but, being independent by nature, she relied on her tractors.

In 1995 Cabot Creamery stopped taking her milk. She was the last one in Vermont, and perhaps New England, to deliver milk to a creamery in milk cans.

"They didn't want to take my milk cans, and they didn't want to send a truck up the hill." Barbara switched to organic farming and now, every other day, a Horizon truck picks up her milk and the company gives her a premium price for the milk.

"I don't know what will happen in the future,

milk prices are so unstable, and costs are high," Barbara says. "What I receive from milk pays my property taxes." Her $12 tax for an old house and 8 acres has escalated to $6,000 for the renovated house, a larger barn she and Charles built, and 340 acres.

Her daughter Barbara, her husband, David, and their new daughter live on the farm and help out. Across the valley, on the farm where her husband grew up, her daughter Mary and her husband, Caleb, raise heifers.

Age has softened Barbara's incredible strength. She now can hoist only 30 pounds of sacked grain where before she hefted 100 pounds and was adept at moving the 83-pound milk cans into the pickup. She still milks and runs the tractor but relies on friends to help out with the haying and sometimes

with the chores. She looks back on the fifty years she dedicated to small-farm living.

"I loved to work in the woods in the winter. I have a lot of horse knowledge that is useless; those days are gone. I like chores. I like hard work.

"The land is what is important and for sure the beauty and the exercise. Cows? They are no more than an economic unit. They come and go. It's the same show but a different cast every year."

Barbara often relaxes in a kitchen chair next to the woodstove. Her face is lined and she suffers from a spinal debility, but she has a sweet smile that reflects a sense of balance between the practical side of working a farm, its beauty, and her life.

"You know, we were all satisfied with less, and I think that is why we survived. Farmers now pay for satellite dishes, fancy tractors, and washing machines, and they expect those things. I am happy with my 1951 International. I don't need a new milking system. I have one old bucket. You can eat only so much.

"You know, I'm out haying or sugaring and I look at the fields and trees and I say, God, it's gorgeous!"

Charlene Rooney — *Maple Sugarer* — ROONEY FARM

Everything changed when Tom was killed," says Charlene, sitting in her kitchen.

"I sugared, cleaned up the barn, took care of the calves, helped with haying. It just never ended." Charlene and David, married since 1970, were also raising their twin daughters, Selina and Siri.

It was five stressful years for the couple. They did not know whether they would have to sell the farm, or part of it, to pay Tom Rooney's family their share of the property. Eventually it was settled, and David and Charlene continue to run the farm. They stopped using the Bull Moose sugarbush, as it was too much work, and they halved the number of taps to 1,500. They reduced the number of milkers from seventy to fifty and switched to organic farming to increase the income from milk. "We were a large farm back then. I guess we are a small farm now."

Their sugarbush is located a couple hundred yards above their farm. The first maples are at about 1,300 feet in elevation, and the grove runs up to 1,600 feet on the side of hill that borders the Vermont State Forest. A beaver meadow is above the bush; the lunch rocks on White Rock overlook the farm and Mud City Loop Road; and an expansive view sweeps down the valley to Morrisville and disappears in the direction of the Northeast Kingdom.

Like most sugarbushes, this one is on the lee side of a mountain, facing south. During sugaring season the wind sings through the upper branches of the maples, while the air remains limpid at the trunks. On a brisk clear day, cumulus clouds, created on the summit of the Sterling Mountain Range, race each other over the treetops. On the ground the snow has

turned to corn and the sap is pinging with staccato verve in the pails. It doesn't take much to work up a sweat in the spring sun, emptying sap buckets. The next day, of course, it could snow.

Charlene couldn't be happier than when she is sugaring on a bright spring day. "The best part of farming is being outdoors, being your own boss, and being around animals. I love animals."

Charlene has two horses, a Morgan and a Quarterhorse, but what she really likes is driving Princess and Sheik, their workhorses, while they are sugaring. She and David take turns driving the horses through the sugarbush and emptying the sap buckets. Sometimes their daughters, Selina and Siri, help. The sap is unloaded into a holding tank that David washes out every time it is emptied. Inside the sugar-

house Norman Kenney, David's brother-in-law, boils the sap, keeps the fire roaring, and fusses over the evaporator. He is as anxious as a day trader as he balances the fire, the temperature in the evaporator, and estimates the instant to draw off the hot syrup.

"We still make fancy syrup, and it is lighter than the samples we get from the state," says Charlene. "David and Norman are finicky about making syrup. But tastes have changed. A lot of the kids don't like the fancy as much as the lower grades with darker color." Some of the Rooney syrup is sold in barrels. The rest Charlene sells out of their home.

Perhaps their fancy syrup, as light as a spring breeze, is so fine because of the way the sap is collected, gathered by horse and sledge from buckets rather than gravity-fed tubes. The altitude of the sugarbush could help — the cold keeps bacteria down in the sap before it is boiled. That however, might change. David has installed plastic tubing to the high reaches of the sugarbush, where sometimes the horses can't get to when there is deep snow. Princess is getting old and in the sugar season of 2002 they had to rent a workhorse to pair up with Sheik. "David is thinking of getting a sled that could be pulled by one horse," says Charlene, "but . . . I don't know . . . David, he is always thinking of how to make farmwork easier."

David is fifty-eight, the average age of a Vermont farmer; Charlene is younger. He had a close call in the winter of 2001, so very similar to his brother's accident. The trunk of the tree he was sawing kicked and spun around, knocked him down, and pinned him to the ground. David thought he had broken his leg, but it turned out to be only a very nasty bruise. This happened on one of the trails in the sugarbush, not far from where Tom was killed fourteen years before.

"It took some finagling for him to get home," Charlene recalls. 'We didn't sugar that spring. David's leg wasn't strong enough . . ." She leaves

unsaid the dark feelings. The accident made them both think about the future.

"I hope David outlives me. He has all the ideas for the farm, and it would be difficult to keep it going. It is really hard labor, and I don't think I could do a lot of it. Selina and Siri both want to keep the farm going, and they live a mile from here.

"I just hope our farm continues. Where I used to live, not far from here, were two farms. One was sold off and there are houses everywhere. The other farm has For Sale signs on their fields. It used to be so beautiful. I would hate to see that happen here. I feel bad about the little farms going out; that was what made Vermont attractive. Now it seems to be a few big farms . . .

"I do want to continue using the horses in the sugarbush."

Sally Goodrich — *Cattle Breeder* — MOLLY BROOK FARMS

She was a queen — haughty, regal, snobbish, vain, egotistic, but then again, what do you expect from such a *grande dame?*

"If someone walked into our barn," said Sally Goodrich, of Molly Brook Farms in North Danville, Vermont, "Fascinator Flower would hold up her head as if to say, 'Don't bother to look at anybody else. Here I am! I'm special — I'm fantastic! I'm better than those other cows! I'm Queen of the Herd!'

"When she was out of the stall she'd pose sideways so people could get a better look. You just can't imagine how regal she was. She and all the Flowers were born with that instinct. It's all in the genes."

Molly Brook Fascinator Flower (1980–1998) was a Jersey cow bred by Sally Goodrich, who in 2002 was recognized nationally as one of America's top breeders of cows.

Fascinator Flower, in her prime, gave more than 22,000 pounds in a milking year (305 days), and her life-time record is 193,000 pounds of milk. She was one of the best milkers in the country with a high butterfat and protein content. She was flat boned and had a big bag, but most important was her ability to transmit her genes. She had twenty-four highly rated daughters and is the dam, grandam, and great-grandam of thirty proven sires — her genes have improved Jersey herds in every continent except Antarctica. Her grandson Flower Power is the best bull in Australia. A granddaughter is milking 110 pounds a day in England and is rated one of that nation's top three Jersey cows. Many cows have the ability to transmit good genes down a generation, but few have the transmittal ability

Fascinator Flower had that has influenced the Jersey breed all over the world.

Sally Goodrich's breeding instinct was at full alert when Fascinator Flower's ma overcame a sickness to return to the milking lineup and produce 60 pounds

of milk with a high butterfat content. "Now that's a sign of greatness in her genes," says Sally, "to have the will to survive an illness and get right up and give so much milk." She decided to breed her to one of the best bulls in America.

The result was Fascinator Flower. "She seemed to be bad luck . . . at first. Fascinator Flower was with her first calf, and it was obvious she was going to be flat in the right-rear quarter. We were going to put her in the Vermont State Sale of 1982 but realized she wouldn't bring much. Who wants to milk a three-teated cow? So we withdrew her from the sale."

After Fascinator Flower gave birth, the teat improved and she yielded copious amounts of milk. She grew into a regal dame, and the rest is history.

Fascinator Flower was Sally Goodrich's great success as a cow woman. She married into a farm, and, on the suggestion of her husband, Walt, she took on the responsibility of improving the herd. She has a sharp instinct for selecting the proper mates but also has a feel for cows. She can remember the names of their ninety-five Jerseys, knows their personalities, and acts as matchmaker. The results are in the family scrapbook, which she shows to visitors. Although she and her husband had six sons, this scrapbook is filled with Molly Brook Farm Jerseys. Her eyes will light up as she recounts the history and personality of her favorite Jerseys as she goes from page to page.

"I have a love for good Jersey cows, heifers, and calves. I have a feel for breeding and I think I was born with it, but because I married a dairy farmer it was brought out.

"I would say I have lived a dream life. I am proud of the sons we have raised. I wanted to learn to fly, and I did that when I was sixty. I wanted to be an outstanding cow woman and Fascinator Flower, ohhh," Sally's eyes light up and she looks up, remembering, "she was superb! Just superb. She was unrivaled by any cow in the world."

Bambi Freeman — *Sheep Farmer* — STERLING BROOK FARM

Bambi's childhood was graciously spent in a proper New Jersey suburb a short trainride from Wall Street, where her father worked as a bond trader. It was an ideal but predictable life of swimming and riding lessons, summer camp, college. But then she took a left turn. She quit college in the mid-1950s to travel, and while on St. Thomas in the Virgin Islands, she met a woman bartender who suggested she could have a good time ski bumming in Vermont — wait on tables and clean rooms for bed and board and a free ski pass.

In the '50s, skiing — particularly ski bumming — was quite an adventure, and Bambi acted on the idea. She found work at a lodge in Stowe that was more fun than work, and besides, there was an abundance of athletic, handsome men on the mountain.

The next year she married David Freeman, a ski patrolman. She was twenty-three.

Bambi held various jobs until she and David founded a hardware store, which endured only long enough for them to become bored behind a counter — four years. In 1970 they bought a very tired home built in 1848. The ramshackle house had been vacant except for a family of porcupines when they and their two children moved in. Dave traded a motorcycle for a pregnant cow. They bought a horse. And then a friend gave them a lamb, which they raised in the house until it was too big for their son to ride. That was the start of Sterling Brook Farm.

The couple increased their acreage to 25, and Bambi raised the sheep. David was a biathlon coach with the U.S. Army and was away most of the

winter. During the summer he did the fieldwork. Within five years they had increased their herd to 150 ewes and spent their days, and some nights too, tending to them — feeding, birthing, arranging for shearing, building fences, and caring for the sick. Every October, through the '70s, Bambi transported many of them to the slaughterhouse and personally delivered the meat to individuals and restaurants. There were some very long days, but they were "Doin' good," as the locals say.

But 1984 and 1985 were dark years for Bambi. In December of 1984 she woke one morning and found she couldn't move; she was paralyzed from the chest down. She was diagnosed with multiple sclerosis, a degenerative disease of the central nervous system. There are two types of the disease, attacking and

progressive. Bambi had the attacking type; she spent six weeks in the hospital and recovered 60 percent of her feeling. At the same time her husband asked for a divorce. In the settlement she received title to the farm but no support for her and her two children.

Coming home to a farm she could not take care of — the sheep had to be sold — and unsure if she would ever be well enough to function normally, Bambi's outlook was bleak. Yet she was to learn of strengths she didn't know she had.

"When I came back from the hospital I was on crutches. I had no balance and no feeling in my legs. It was like I was on Novocaine. I could get to the barn, but I was slower than death. You know what it is like to hobble on crutches over an icy path in the dark of a winter morning?

"A neurological physical therapist programmed me to relearn to crawl on my belly, and then on my hands and knees. I had a mat in the basement and I would go down the stairs on my bum and then crawl around on the mat. The dentist I worked for, who helped greatly with disability payments, lent me his rowing machine, and that put me back in shape. Finally I could walk with two canes. Then one. Then none. But I had no reflexes on my right side. I couldn't feel and had to teach myself again how to use my hands and feet — to use knitting needles I had to look at them and tell them what to do. I learned to be very focused on all my manual chores,

particularly when I climb up and down the hayloft. I have to be aware of cold and heat. A doctor who tested me later was dumbfounded. He said I should be in a wheelchair."

In 1985 she began to reconstruct her life as a farmer and a mother. She bought a "retirement flock" of nine sheep and returned to doing chores. It focused her, and she found that a visit to her dogs and sheep in the barn lifted her from depression. Her most important revelation, after the divorce and the return of her flock, was about herself.

"I realized that when I was married I shared half the credit for the farm, but I took full responsibility if something went wrong because I was the one doing it. After my divorce I didn't have to share the credit, and that changed my life. I had self-esteem

and I knew, from that point on, MS or not, that I was not the same person as before. It was an eye opener to me. It is so important to build up self-esteem and to feel successful when you are knocked down and come back up."

In the years since, Bambi has increased the size of the herd and selected breeds of sheep known to birth multiple lambs, so she has more lambs to market. She has developed value-added products, knitting wool hats and sweaters and having her sheepskins tanned. A centuries-old company in Michigan makes duvets and bed liners from her wool. She continues to work three part-time jobs, and she sells directly to her customers and through farmers' markets. Bambi has also learned to expect no help from the state agricultural department.

"They teach us small-animal farmers self-reliance, for in this state, if it doesn't moo, it doesn't count."

Bambi recently learned from another farmer in Virginia how to raise chickens in portable sheds in which twenty-five chickens can roost. She moves them from the lawn to the sheep paddock to the garden. Last summer she raised 225 free-range chickens and marketed them after seven and a half weeks.

"People come to me at farmers' market and ask if I ship, and I tell them no. I tell them to come back to Vermont and bring their cooler. People visit our state because our products are unique, that's why they buy my lamb meat and chickens, my sheep skins, blankets, duvets, and hats. I would rather sell to one person ten different products than sell one hundred people one product. To be small like me you have to market yourself, otherwise the middleman will take your profits."

Bambi has no checking account; she pays by bank check and cash. She has no mortgage. She has a credit card herself but does not accept them at the farmers' markets (she tells customers where the nearest ATM is). People call in an order to her house and she puts it in a cooler on the porch and they leave a check. Her only hobby, if it could be called that, is training her Border collies, Galen and Roy, and her gregarious old-world guard dog, Yugo, who recently treed a black bear that ambled too close to the sheep paddock.

"It is a wonderful sense of accomplishment and pride for me to make this farm work. It became very important to rebuild my barn and keep it in good shape, to put a new roof on my house, to add an artesian well, to paint my tractor."

Bambi has given talks to single mothers in her region about how growing produce for their families creates independence and self-esteem, as it did for her.

"Women are perfect to be on the land," she says. "They are industrious, they don't mind working in the dirt and raising food, they feel good about themselves, and their children like to help out."

Bambi was voted Farmer of the Year in 2000 by her regional Conservation District. It was the first time a non-cow person, and a woman, was selected.

Pat Goodall — *Emu Farmer* — Borderline Ratites Farm

My husband, he went over to fix a large furnace in his mother's house. He had just cleaned the manure spreader with diesel fuel and had it all over his clothes, and when he went down to the cellar, a back draft from the furnace set him on fire. Well, he survived that but they did a routine X-ray and found he had cancer. They gave him chemotherapy, and it killed him.

"Rudy and I worked this farm that had been in the Goodall family for one hundred years. We milked 110 Holsteins. No matter how bad the days were, there was always something to laugh about, but after he died it was no fun anymore. I was putting in sixteen to eighteen hours a day. I had to hire help, and I lost money faster than I made it. I kept the farm going for about ten months, then I sold the cows, the machinery, and part of the farmland."

Pat Goodall is a stubborn, tough, self-deprecating farmer brought up in the Northeast Kingdom of Vermont. She smokes cigarettes as if she were French, and she talks bluntly. Like most Vermont-reared farmers, she is curious and relies on common sense.

"So what was I to do after I sold the herd? I didn't want to punch a time clock for anybody. I thought about getting sheep, then goats or pigs, but I didn't see making a living off them. Then I looked at emus, and I said to myself, 'Now that is something totally different. I need a challenge, I need something I can put my teeth into and learn.'

"That was 1994. I've proven that and then some."

As many as 175 emus have been penned in very high fences on Pat's Borderline Ratites Farm in Derby, Vermont, just a holler from the Canadian border. She is one of seven Vermont farmers who have banded together to form Vermont Prime Emu Producers. They market meat, but more important to their bottom line is emu oil.

Emus evolved over the past 80 million years in Australia and so, naturally, are their national bird. An emu stands just under 6 feet and weighs about 120 pounds, second in size only to the ostrich. Like all ratite birds, the emu cannot fly, but it is a fierce runner; 9-foot strides can move the bird up to 35 mph. It is a fierce and dangerous kicker; an emu would make a heck of a rugby player.

The skin of the emu is used for leather. The meat is low in cholesterol and fat, red in color. Like venison, emu meat is tasty when cooked rare but tastes like a rubber tire if it is overcooked. Emu oil, though, is an antidote used by the Australian Aborigines for cuts, bruises, and other ailments. Rendered from the fat of the bird, it is clear and colorless and has curative powers that many people swear by, although some doctors consider it no more than a folk cure.

The oil is a highly penetrating mixture of fatty acids that can be synthesized by the human body. Historically, the emu produced the oil to lubricate its skin and muscles in Australia's searing outback, and for years humans have recognized it as a moisturizer that relieves acne and eczema. When mixed with wintergreen and eucalyptus, it reduces inflammation of muscles and joints; new studies indicate it lessens swelling and pain from arthritis. Some people ingest it in capsules to help lower cholesterol.

"Those 1,200-pound Holsteins I handled for years abused my back, and I have arthritis of the spine," says Pat. "I couldn't carry one 50-pound grain bag across the barnyard. Now I take four emu gelcaps a day, and after two years I can take four or five bags across the yard. My spine still hurts, but it's livable."

It didn't help when one of her emus gave her a kick and sent her flying 10 feet in the air. They are dangerous and as wild as a buffalo.

"Emus are all feet and legs. Their three toenails are like razor blades, and they can rip you to shreds. A kick can snap a bone like nothing. You have to handle them from the rear. We have a harness that we put on some birds. Others go crazy if we try to use it on them."

Australia no longer allows emus to be exported, so many of the birds now come from zoo stock. Pat has mixed her flock with emus from France, and the birds have adapted well to Vermont's cold weather.

In the early 1990s the emu became trendy; the price of a breeder pair of emus went as high as $60,000, and an egg was worth $1,000. There were some bad scams, and then the shell game went bust.

"They just thought of money and didn't do their homework," Pat says. "I'm trying to make a living, but in the process I try to help people so they don't have to use drugs and steroids. One lady wrote me that she suffered from eczema so bad she had deformed fingernails and didn't want to shake hands with people. The oil cleaned up her eczema, and now she can polish her nails and feel feminine. A letter like that makes me feel good.

"I learn something about my birds every day. People stop here and ask questions. I interact with them, and that has been good. Otherwise I would be more inclined to hibernate, to insulate myself. And I'm too young to do that."

Lydia Ratcliff — *Goat Farmer* — Lovejoy Brook Farm

Lydia Ratcliff is a sixty-nine-year-old goat farmer who operates the Lovejoy Brook Farm in Andover, Vermont, home to herself, one hundred goats and sheep, and a few cows and calves. To some she is known as an eccentric, suffering from emphysema and arthritis, who bottle-nurses kids in her kitchen and operates an on-the-edge farm. To others Lydia is a hard-nosed, inflexible autocrat in the way she runs the enterprises she has created, but any way you look at it, Lydia is a brilliant intellectual, propagator of small-farm diversity who knows how to manipulate the market to the advantage of the farmers she works with. She is a New York native, a college graduate fluent in French and Italian, a former researcher for *Time* magazine and the columnist Sylvia Porter, whose financial column reached 40 million Americans in the 1970s. Lydia ghosted most of *Sylvia Porter's Money Book,* which became a best seller in 1975. She took her portion of the royalties and left New York City for Vermont to establish her goat farm. She continues to do research — sometimes freelance, sometimes for herself, and most often on the subject of small-farm viability, which is her primary interest.

Lydia started Vermont Quality Meats and Fancy Meats from Vermont, two cooperatives (why two?— politics) that deliver lambs, goat, pigs, veal, venison, game birds, chickens, and eggs to the best restaurants in Boston and New York, including Daniel, Lutèce, Union Square Café, Chanterelle, and Gramercy Tavern, among others. She also organized Northeast Dairy Associates, which has exported live goats and semen from New England farms to Vietnam, Taiwan, and Israel. New England livestock is considered valuable by international breeders because of its genetics and disease-free condition.

The following quotations are from two interviews held with Lydia in her Andover home. Some of her comments refer to her personal life as a farmer, others to the state of farming in Vermont.

"The more successful small farms have a wife to care for the house and children to help with milking and feeding calves. The farm is always free and clear, and the farmer makes do with old equipment that he upgrades judiciously. He has improved his herd with artificial insemination. I didn't have this farm free and clear, I didn't have the husband to do most of

the work, and I didn't have the sons and family to help out or lean on, and besides, I didn't know anything about farming. I bought my first mower because it was freshly painted and it looked red and nice. But it didn't work."

"The coming global famine will be the result not of the decline of the breadbasket, or its depletion, but the loss, from development and misuse, of marginal agricultural lands, which is all of New England. My concern is the small farms. Why don't local stores buy from local producers? Why don't our schools buy locally? They don't because the mass producers can do it a few cents cheaper. It is canned or frozen or grown on huge farms and transported thousands of miles, and God knows what you are eating."

"An auctioneer says, 'It would be a good herd if fed up.' I see that in auction notices all the time. They try to put a positive light on it. The fact is that the farmer has to cut corners. Income is down, and the farmer is pushed over the line, so the herd is not well fed."

"Crowding is the worst sin — crowding of people and animals. I came up to Vermont to get away from crowding. I went from a high income to a sub-poverty income after the royalties ran out [on *Sylvia Porter's Money Book*]. That is not a disadvantage. I think it is more admirable to be poor than rich. I enjoy having no money more than a lot of money, or I should say I certainly was not happier with a lot of money. I am my own boss; I'm in better physical shape except for emphysema. I do what I like, and 90 percent of

Americans do not like what they are doing. When people or animals are concentrated, one of the results is a large mass of money. Then the people fight tooth and nail for their portion. In the country it is the environment that loses out in this fight."

"We are asking our livestock to pay for a lot more than they used to. They didn't have to pay for TV, washing machines, VCRs, or better cars and trucks and 40,000-dollar tractors. Property taxes and health insurance are decimating us. It didn't make the headlines, but the national medical costs just crossed the trillion-dollar mark."

"I was first shaken by the environmental alarms of the late 1960s when Rachel Carson wrote her book, *Silent Spring*. First I wanted to get solar panels and unhitch myself from electricity and cars. The right thing to do was to work in my own backyard, to keep the soil fertile on my farm, and badger the owners of other farms in the area to not let their fields grow over and to spread manure and fence them. The topsoil in Vermont is down to less than 3 inches on the average. It will not sustain much if manure or nutrients are not put in it; there will no longer be green pastures. More horse farms are coming into Vermont, and they don't put horse or cow manure on their land. The large, free-stall farms have huge manure pits and are milk factories; their cows do not go out to graze and fertilize the fields. That is creating a disaster."

"Vermont farmers have done more to make Vermont beautiful and keep it that way than any other people — but those who benefit financially from that beauty are the resort operators, the bankers, the building-trades people, the real-estate agents and developers, and so on. People come to Vermont as tourists to see a scenery enhanced by farmers, yet banks won't give mortgages to farms because they are 'bad risks.' But these same banks are cashing in on the tourist trade and second-home market. The result is that farms are lost in the shuffle and dying like flies and no one is throwing them a bone. In some countries the governments sustain small farms, give them a pension and help them buy equipment. I think we should have a bank program for small farmers. It could be called a Thank You Grant given to deserving small farmers for doing a good job, and they must be in some need but not on the brink of bankruptcy. Say the banks allocated $50,000 to that program and fifty farmers would get $1,000 each, no strings attached. Think of the advertising value of that — the banks could say, 'We are proud to announce that we gave away $1,000 each to the following farmers for keeping Vermont beautiful by staying in business.' It's the least we can do for those who are enriching all of our lives."

"Goats are the most charming of animals; it's a disease you catch, they get under your skin. Dairy farmers call them second-class cows, and I tell them goats can outperform cows for milk. Did you ever hear of Goat Widows? It's a serious problem. Husbands get jealous of the wives' devotion to the goats and so they get a goat divorce. The wife is too involved with the goats, and it is the other way around too."

"Our slaughterhouses are being overregulated and there are fewer and fewer of them. There is a big difference between the regulations needed for a huge meat-packing plant and a small one in Vermont. The New York chefs want clean, wholesome, fresh, nonmedicated Vermont products, and they will pay us more for it. But if we can't get it slaughtered and inspected, these chefs can't buy it, and that might be the death knell of many small farms."

"Small farmers need to sell direct. It is the difference between making a little money and losing a lot. Five dollars a pound for a whole animal is good. The chef charges $30 for an entrée, and they are happy to pay $5 a pound for the meat in that entrée."

"There are a lot of hobby farmers, or checkbook farmers, who donate their land to the Vermont Land Trust. Part of my land is in their trust, but I would rather leave the farm to a younger person living in a little cottage down the road. I don't want to leave the farm to someone to make a killing; I want someone to continue this way of life."

"The world is a very troubling place and the news is constantly assaulting our sanity. There needs to be some sort of stabilizing force in our lives in the absence of extended family. It's important to do everyday things that are not too demanding physically or mentally, such as watering houseplants, feeding calves, milking or weeding the garden. It takes your mind off the troubles of the world, and it also involves productive work."

"Goats eat shingles off the sides of barns; they eat wooden fences. Sometimes I think you need a goat carpenter to invent fences they can't get out of."

"Everybody looks at the GNP as a gauge of economic success, but there is a more sensible way to design a GNP to measure progress. Fifty atomic bombs made is not progress, yet it is part of the GNP. The GNP fails to measure aesthetics or environmental benefits."

"The meat and semen businesses that I am involved with give value-added income to small farms. People who sell internationally young bred goats or bucks receive two to three times as much for those animals as they would from local markets. Semen sells for $15 a straw. This extra income helps a small farmer make ends meet."

"The Vermont Department of Agriculture gives us the bare minimum, just the crumbs from an affluent table. They like cows. Most of the federal grant money they receive they siphon off to bureaucrats and consultants who don't know the first thing about the problems we face as farmers. Very little of it comes to us."

"The basic thing for small farmers is to survive in Vermont, which is essentially a poor agricultural state — poor in the sense of soil richness and growing season and topography. We can't grow big and compete with Iowa, which has free corn to feed their animals. We have to sell a different size, a different breed, to a different market and do something different so that people will pay $5, rather than $1, a pound."

"What makes a good farmer? It's a calling. You have to be close to the line, very frugal, and not have extras. You use old equipment, don't take vacations, and drive an old car. Your house needs paint, and forget about eating out.

"There is sadness and frustration too. I spent most of my life making this farm sing in one way or the other, and then, in my older age, I see it fall down around me. You feel helpless and a failure if your place is dying and decrepit. Sometimes I feel that way and think I can't cope with it. I'd like to go out with the same busy, working farm with repairs caught up, not just a shambles of broken stuff with junk all over. How can you have pride for your life's work if it looks a mess? You don't have the money and any you have you use to buy your medicine or inhalers or a square meal or pay property taxes. You have to pay that, you don't have to have the shed repaired or fix the leaky roof. Those can wait, property taxes don't. Running a farm is more than making money. You put your heart and soul into a farm. You work very hard to make it go, to make it survive for as long as you can.

"Yeahhh, I like to play in the dirt. I garden barefoot and I get really dirty and I dig with my hands and I just love it," and she gives that big smile and her eyes light up. Karen has a smooth face, a happy smile, and a way that makes you want to open up to her, to confide those everyday doubts common to us all. She is an Earth Mother.

"When we moved in, I was overwhelmed by the openness and space around the house. I walked around the lawn at different times of the day, to get an idea of what and where to plant. It was almost like the plants told me where they wanted to be or the trees knew where they wanted to grow."

Her husband, Charlie, was a truck driver who spent ninety to one hundred hours a week delivering grain from their home in Connecticut to Vermont farms where he saw husbands, wives, and their kids working together. Tired of trucking and starved for a family life, he told his wife what he found in Vermont. In 1983 they sold their farm and health food store in Connecticut, and they, their two children, furniture, and three carloads of family plants — some generations old ("We looked like a traveling jungle," says Karen), moved in to this old house on 89 acres in Whiting. They bought it because Charlie loved the barn and Karen liked the peonies and the lace curtains in the house. They named their farm Popoma, bought a herd of Jerseys, and soon were milking forty-five. Karen became barefoot in the garden.

Her flower garden is divided into two sections. The Moon Garden is planted with silver and white flowers, which stand out so well in moonlight. The Sun Garden is filled with orange and red flowers and glows like fire when lit by the sun. Within the decorative flowers in this garden are many varieties of herbs. A swath of grass separates the vegetable garden, velvety in deep green leaf on this July day.

Karen gives away cut flowers and vegetables; she refuses to sell them. "Giving makes me feel wealthy," she says, but on her computer are three different businesses — supplying cut flowers for weddings; creating dried flower wreaths and compounding herbal potions; and teaching — tutoring children with learning problems and filling in as a substitute teacher.

The attic, murky and shadowy, looks at first glance like a bat den, but it is only clumps of drying herbs and flowers hanging from the rafters. In a corner under a bare bulb Karen makes her wreaths. They are ordered for weddings, birthdays, anniversaries, new babies, house warmings, and Christmas. Karen is working on a wreath for a wedding.

"The herbs that I chose for this wreath are artemsia, which is named after Artemis, the goddess of the moon and the hunt who protects young animals. So the meaning is protection. Marjoram represents joy and happiness. I put in thyme for courage and strength. The sage is the symbol of a happy family life and laughter. Lavender is for devotion. Roses of course show love. I also add larkspur. It doesn't have its own meaning but it is incredibly beautiful, so the meaning is appreciation

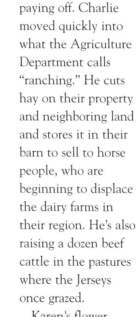

of beauty, which is very important for a marriage. Then I write a little tag that lists the flowers and what they mean."

Karen also makes potions from her herbs. She emphasizes that she is not a healer but has an extensive library of information. She concocts a balm from comfrey, olive oil, beeswax, and tea tree oil that may be applied to cuts, bruises, burns, and skin problems. She mixes St. John's wort with eucalyptus, lavender, thyme, and white pine oils for stiff muscles. Sage and

chickweed make an effective insect sting ointment. Catnip tea is for an upset stomach, headaches and nervous tension. If someone has a particular problem, she will do the research, gather the necessary herbs from the garden, and make the remedy.

The dairy part of the farm lasted longer than it should have, for dairy farming is a risky sport in Vermont. In 2000 they sold their herd; it wasn't paying off. Charlie moved quickly into what the Agriculture Department calls "ranching." He cuts hay on their property and neighboring land and stores it in their barn to sell to horse people, who are beginning to displace the dairy farms in their region. He's also raising a dozen beef cattle in the pastures where the Jerseys once grazed.

Karen's flower business pays for the property taxes and health insurance. They grow most of their food and cut firewood to feed their two woodstoves. The haying and tutoring puts them over the top.

Summertime is Karen's joy. When the delphiniums stand tall and gloriously opulent in blue, she holds an open house to celebrate the beauty of the coming summer.

"I like being with the earth and in the sunshine, creating beauty. The garden satisfies all those things.

It is important to be connected with the land and the weather. I enjoy my neighbors who are now our friends. This life in Vermont strengthened our family and has been wonderful for our kids. Now that our children are grown, we take in children from other families. While they stay with us we do not allow them to watch television during the day or play video games or other electronic devices. We teach them to pick up after themselves, to do chores, to eat well and if they want to play in mud puddles it's okay to be filthy, stinking dirty. They make hay forts or play with the kittens or skip down to the pond and catch frogs."

Karen is one of those people whose sensitivity responds to other levels of consciousness.

"I think a lot of very good people have lived here, in this house and on this land, and their good vibes have lingered [supposedly Samuel Beech, a Green Mountain boy and friend of Ethan Allen, who rounded up the troops to take Fort Ticonderoga, lived on the property]. It is protected, almost like a sanctuary. I am sure that's one reason why we were drawn to this place."

Annette Smith — *Sustainable Farmer and Activist* — BLUE BEECH FARM

Annette Smith's goal was to grow most of her own food and live on less than $5,000 a year. After eleven years of building up her small farm, she found that her 50 acres were in the middle of a couple of billion-dollar projects: a proposed pipeline supported by a group of North American corporate companies that would connect two planned electrical plants, and an open mining pit owned by a company that operates in thirty countries and is privately controlled by a Swiss billionaire. So here you have a woman whose life and tranquillity, and those of her neighbors and the rural valley they live in, is about to be squashed. What does she do?

"When you're cleaning other people's toilets, you have time to think about what you really want to do," says Annette Smith. It was the 1980s and the toilets she was cleaning were in the homes of the affluent near Boston, Massachusetts. She came up with a list of what she wanted for a home:

- 50 acres of land
- A cabin
- Water, electricity, or toilet, but not necessarily all three
- View is not important
- Freedom and privacy

In 1987 she bought a cabin with water and septic but no electricity on a 50-acre patch of a rural agricultural valley in Danby, Vermont. Annette had lived in New Hampshire and Maine and found them wanting. "Vermont was the last bastion of freedom. It had the reputation of leaving people alone and letting them do their own thing. I felt that when I came here."

She hadn't always wanted to farm, although her ancestors worked a small farm in Pennsylvania. She is a first-class violinist (her mother was a musical child prodigy) and at one point she was building harpsichords, which was a light-hearted time in her life — she was photographed in the nude on one of them.

Annette planned to grow fruit and vegetables and raise livestock to sustain herself. She wanted to garden according to the precepts of *biodynamics*, a system developed by Rudolf Steiner (Austrian, 1861–1925), a philosopher, artist, architect, scientist, and educator who founded Anthroposophy, a path of knowledge that guides the spiritual nature of

the human being with the cosmic strength of the universe. In a series of lectures in 1924 Steiner laid out the elements of biodynamic horticulture, which is the oldest organic system of gardening. Biodynamic gardeners use homeopathic potions that create vigorous life in soil, plants, and animals. They follow a time table for planting and fertilizing the soil in conjunction with planetary forces.

What Annette didn't know was that she'd bought an old gravel pit and would have to create soil before she could do any farming at all. She purchased a cow and a mule, chickens, and one duck and began making compost. She used a crowbar and a shovel to pry the rocks apart so she could plant fruit trees and made beds of compost to grow her first vegetables. She installed solar panels for electricity and used propane to run her stove and

refrigerator. Her water is gravity fed from a nearby spring.

Slowly, her farm took root. She now has eighty free-range chickens and sells eggs to a health food store in Manchester. There are geese and a beef cow, a Jersey cow whose milk is made into yogurt, butter, and cottage cheese with enough left over to drink. Thirty-five varieties of apple trees decorate the former gravel pit, and there are also lemon, lime, cherry, apricot, plum, peach, and pear trees. Raspberry, blueberry, and currant bushes; grapes; horseradish; and an asparagus bed are interspersed among the fruit trees. Her garden supplies all her vegetables. In the spring she boils enough maple sap to last the year, and in the summer she raises a couple of pigs.

She found that she could live on $5,000 a year, of which $2,600 was spent on grain. She made wooden boxes, lawn furniture from copper tubing, and intricate seamstress work to pay for her sugar, coffee, paper, and other necessities.

It was in 1998 that she read in the newspaper about a projected 1,000-megawatt power plant to be built in Rutland. It would have emissions so clean it would be nothing but water vapor and carbon dioxide, reported a spokesman for the plant. "This is not true," Annette said to herself, and she went online to do some research.

"I became obsessed about learning more about energy and what was proposed for Rutland." She shortly found out that two natural gas electrical plants were planned, one in Rutland and another in Bennington, that they would generate 1,300 megawatts of energy, while Vermont doesn't use more than 650 megawatts a year (on average), that the burning of the fossil fuels would lead to pollution. Then she found out that a natural gas pipeline would be built from out of state to the electrical plants, and the pipeline would cross her property.

She eventually understood that energy companies were planning to build fifty-six plants in New England, that the power generated by the proposed Vermont plants was to be sold out of Vermont, that the pipeline was a conduit for gas to be transported to New Hampshire, Maine, and Massachusetts, and because there would be an anticipated demand for more natural gas than is available, the cost for natural gas would sky rocket.

"Vermont was not going to benefit," Annette says as she sits next to the brook that runs through her property. She is brown eyed with straight hair, a dead-level look worthy of a good poker player, and a bemused sense of self-irony. "The power plants would be using millions of gallons of water a day, wetlands were endangered by the pipeline. There was a pollution factor because both Bennington and Rutland are centered in geographical bowls and prone to inversion. Worst of all, the pipeline would be laid through a dozen towns, most of them small rural communities between Rutland and Bennington."

The electrical plants and pipeline project seemed to be a done deal; it had the backing of the Vermont governor and local business booster groups. Property owners and town selectmen were being asked to support it. That is when Annette began visiting and talking to selectmen of ten communities and reporting to them what sort of impact the electrical plants and pipeline would have on Vermont and their small towns. They listened and nine voted locally against the pipeline. Annette was so effective that Vermonters for a Clean Environment, a nonprofit group, was organized, and she became the executive director. She organized the towns and landowners and put up a fierce fight against the power plants and the pipeline. She asked property owners to send notices of no trespassing to state officials and pipeline employees. She then found that some politicians were trying to change Act 248, the

energy law that protects the public good, so that the pipeline and plants could be built. So much community effort went into protecting their towns and lifestyle that Governor Dean, who had admonished people to get behind the project, abandoned his support of the plants and pipeline. The project never even filed for the permits necessary, and by the end of 2000 the electrical plants and the pipeline were as dead as a couple of skunks in the road.

"It was a harsh, two-year fight," recalls Annette. "I remember coming outside after milking the cow and looking up. I live in this big bowl rimmed by trees and mountains. The stars were particularly bright, and it was so beautiful and quiet. I thought that now I could concentrate on my seeds and regenerating the soil."

OMYA, Inc., is a subsidiary of the private company Pluess-Staufer Industries of Oftringen, Switzerland. The company has 140 plants in thirty countries, which grind marble into calcium carbonate. In Vermont they have quarries in Middlebury, Florence, and South Wallingford and a plant in Florence where the marble is mixed with water and crushed into calcium carbonate slurry. The calcium carbonate is used as a whitener in magazine paper (*National Geographic* is 40 percent calcium carbonate) floor tiles, carpet backing, joint compound, PVC pipe, tooth paste, even Tums.

In December of 1999, a geologist for OMYA approached the town of Tinmouth's selectboard and planning commission and asked what they would

think of OMYA opening an open-pit mine on Dutch Hill south of the town. Forty trucks would carry the crushed rock from Danby through Tinmouth to Wallingford and Route 7 and then go to their crushing plant in Florence. OMYA did not receive the best reception. It turned out that there was a connection between the natural gas pipeline and OMYA, who wanted to install a slurry pipeline next to the natural gas line. Annette Smith's success in blocking the natural gas line and the electric-generating plants had put a crimp in their plans. But not for long.

"OMYA is a big and scarier monster," says Annette. "They own a mile and a half of scenic mountain that is in the center of one of Vermont's most photographed scenes. They want to blast a 35-acre (to 'start small') open pit into that view. The pit, called the Jobe Phillips Quarry, would be just about a mile away from me. The blast from an open-pit mine is sixty times stronger than a blast in a traditional quarry (fabrication block). The trucks they intend to use — 75,000-pound 18 wheelers — would go past my property. This is a small, rural valley. We have coexisted with an underground marble quarry (in Danby), but exploding the hillside and trucking this marble to a crushing plant would ruin our life and our valley."

OMYA's owner is Max Schachenmann, a Swiss national who was recognized as a billionaire in 1992 by *Fortune Magazine*. There is very little information on him or the value of his companies. He is also known as Mr. Silent. What can be gleaned from some international reports is that his policy for OMYA is to open worldwide as many marble quarries and calcium carbonate crushing plants as possible; to create, through research, more use for the product and to corner the market. To such ends OMYA has been brutal in forcing their operations into towns that did not want mining operations. In France their intrusion into Vingrau, a wine-producing town in the Pyrenees, led to hunger strikes and violence. Eighty-five percent of the town opposed the quarry and marble-crushing plant, yet OMYA threatened to move all their operations out of France unless they received permission to mine in Vingrau. The French government allowed them to proceed; the people of Vingrau had no power to stop a global company from doing whatever it wanted within their town. Similar fights against OMYA, but not as violent, are taking place in other countries, including Canada.

"What OMYA wants to do is take apart a beautiful Vermont mountain and turn it into paper." Annette pulls no punches. "My job is becoming more and more clear. It is about protecting our valley, our towns and way of life. Is it right for them to come in and ruin our quality of life, to create noise and dust and traffic and to have this mountain and valley destroyed forever? Is it right for us to lose our property value?

"OMYA is the largest user of pesticides in Vermont, but they also are the largest carriers on Vermont Railway. Their general philosophy is that they own the land and the rights to it and they have a right to mine and truck their stone out and crush it, and they don't care what you want or think; they are going ahead and if you don't like it, move away."

Annette works in the living room of her cabin. Around the cabin it looks a bit like Appalachia, unpainted, roughly fenced. There is an old tub on edge with no Madonna in it, some Cadillac hubcaps are fastened to the side of the cabin, as is a National Rifle Association logo and a sign to watch out for the dogs. There is a shotgun by the door and inside some patched targets. On the kitchen table is a Mac computer and stacks of documents. Books overflow the shelves. Annette sits at the table in front of her computer, with a phone headset covering her ears, researching facts to use as ammunition in her releases for Vermonters for a Clean Environment. Her home is also the group's office.

But her involvement has created a large stress factor. She has been threatened, her mail box destroyed; she has been harassed by individuals and groups. She now spends more time working as executive director than in her garden. Her VCE salary of $36,000 blew away her subsistence dreams of $5,000 a year, but what the heck, there has to be some trade offs. "I was going to buy new solar panels but income tax took what I saved. I tell you, I would much rather just tend to my garden. This is a devastating fight.

"Remember that I said Vermont is a bastion of freedom? Right now I see Vermont as a block of Swiss Cheese. All wrapped up it looks and feels solid, but take off the wrapping and you find these giant holes that nobody sees or talks about. It's not as free a state as when I moved here.

"The killed pipeline and electrical plants and the

The proposed OMYA open pit mine would be in the middle of one of Vermont's favorite scenes — the valley and mountains surrounding Danby Four Corners and Tinmouth. The quarry would be in the upper center of this photograph, in the area that has been clear-cut.

placing of mining quarries in unique, rural communities brings up important questions for all people who choose to live in sparsely populated areas. What is important to us? The perception is that Vermont is an environmental state and we have clean air and water. Another perception is that it is a damned hard place to make a living, but for me and my neighbors we care about the quality of life rather than having a fat bank account."

Perhaps Annette Smith happens to be in the wrong place at the wrong time. Or is it the right place at the right time? Is Vermont broaching from a rural state to a factory economy? Is the government of Vermont going to support the corporate balance sheet over a town's desire? Is it right to take a small region of Vermont, say Annette Smith's sub-

sistence farm, and bombard it with dust and noise and perhaps ruin her water supply and diminish her own investment? What sort of triage is the average Vermonter willing to take in the trade-off between industry jobs, the environment, and people's peace of mind?

In the meantime, during the summer of 2002, Annette's Jersey, Lilac, had a calf, which she named Lily of the Valley, for the flowers that were in bloom when she was born. Red the mule is as shy as ever; it is his manure that helps grow the cabbages, potatoes, and asparagus that Annette was dining on in the spring, along with homegrown beef, raspberry ice cream, and lemon pudding — all raised on her farm. She just picked up a pair of piglets. Her pet chicken, Quinn, who is in her eighth year, developed asthma

and now has her own oxygen supply. Voles have been eating her peas, spinach, and onions, but she has found castor oil solves the problem. More of her apple trees bloomed this year than ever before, and she believes it is because she is spraying them with kaolin clay, which keeps the curculio weevils away (ironically, OMYA's calcium carbonate is replacing kaolin as the mineral filler in paper). Bluebirds and Baltimore orioles are nesting in her garden, and on one afternoon a pileated woodpecker flew over her property.

Annette's elderly friends and family are having health problems, a warning for her to keep the right perspective about what's important in life, but she realizes that the silence and tranquillity of their valley can be snuffed out forever by an international conglomerate. And that's not right.

Mary Beth Fischer — *Pig and Cattle Farmer* — FISCHER FARM

M y goal is a sustainable farm — a small farm that feeds my family, a few neighbors, and pays for itself. I'm almost there," says Mary Beth Fischer. Her farm is small, hidden on a back road in West Springfield. "I do fencing to make up the difference."

Mary Beth has eight sows that deliver annually about eight pigs each, forty cattle, a crossbreed milker, a flock of chickens, and a horse. She worked as a hired farmhand for eight years in the Albany area and found she was happiest working outside and with animals. When she and her husband, Richard, a backhoe and bulldozer operator, moved to Vermont to escape urbanization, she started her farm, and he slowly built up his earth-moving business.

Most of her produce is sold locally. The crossbreed cow provides milk for her family and a friend who lives down the road. About five steers are butchered each year and sold to locals. Pigs are usually sold in the spring, and neighbors fatten them up for slaughter in the fall.

"I like the idea of selling to locals. Many of my customers want to know exactly what my cattle are fed, and so they come over and see. Sometimes I have to show them where they sleep. I feed the pigs nothing but grain. I tried other things — rice cakes, that had little nutrition, stale bread, even Ben & Jerry's ice-cream waste — but nothing worked as well as grain. My beef cattle are given no additives, just hay and grain. I start them on cornmeal, hay, and silage, then they are pastured. I finish them off with 25 pounds of corn a day — people still like

that marbled taste of corn-fattened beef. I'm my own best customer, and if I don't like it, I don't grow it."

What will happen in the future to this sustainable farm remains uncertain. Mary Beth has more than enough energy and strength to run it for another twenty-five years, health permitting. Her daughter Rachel was once interested in farm animals and was training a pair of steers but had to make a choice between steers and boyfriends — boyfriends won out. She now wants to be a graphic designer. Her youngest daughter Alise is not wild about farm animals — she hopes to be a dolphin trainer. Alise often brings her friend Annette to the farm; she loves animals and shadows Mary Beth as she feeds her stock, castrates them, gives them shots. Perhaps she will grow up to work with animals.

"What I do is local to local," says Mary Beth, "and it's fun growing produce that people feel good about eating and not wondering where it came from. I enjoy it. I'm an outdoor person and hate doing anything inside. And, yes, I do like to dig fence holes."

Blanche Jarvis — *Matriarch* — Jarvis Farm

The hospital bed with its side railing up is centered in the old dining room. Upon it lies Blanche Jarvis. Her sore-covered feet, wrapped in gauze, stuck out from under a light coverlet. She is as still as death but her good blue eye is open and roaming the room. She breathes through her toothless mouth; for the past three and a half years she hasn't had to chew, as her daughter Sylvia spoonfeeds her with baby food. Beside her bed is a cast-iron woodstove. On the side wall, above a cabinet of knickknacks, a handmade poster shouts in bold letters of red and blue: *Happy 104th Birthday*. Behind and above the bed, stark against the wall, Jesus walks on a rectangle of black velvet, carrying the Cross. Opposite the end of the bed and seated on a sofa squeezed between heaps of magazines and boxes is Leonard Jarvis, eighty-one, her fourth child. His sister Sylvia, sixty-seven, leans against the doorjamb. Behind her is the kitchen. Curiously, there is no smell in this room. It is a summer day in July, 2001.

Blanche can barely hear and talk; her son and daughter are here to translate for me. I have set up a microphone on a tripod facing Leonard, who has placed himself in the center of a sofa. I sit in a chair facing the bed with the recorder on my lap. The furniture, the bed, the boxes, and the stove cramp the room.

Leonard talks slowly and precisely. For twenty-six years he worked for Pratt and Whitney in Connecticut. In World War II he was a bombardier in a B24 outfit stationed in Africa, and before that he was a farm kid, born in this house. His home is within tractor distance, and he rode over on one this morning. Sylvia and Frances, her husband, and

her mother live in this old family farmhouse, at the end of Jarvis Road, on a hill above East Braintree.

"This farm has been in the family eighty-four, eighty-five years," says Leonard. "All we ever called it was the Jarvis Farm. Mom was twenty-two when I was born — right here in this house. And so was Sylvia. Mom had nine children and she lost three. I know what that is like. The older you get, the more the mind is taken care of, so the losses don't bother as much."

"MOM HAD A BROKEN LEG. IN FACT BOTH LEGS WERE BAD . . . THOUGHT THEY WOULD HAVE TO BE AMPUTATED, BUT THEY'RE OKAY NOW," Sylvia yells from the kitchen. Her voice penetrates like a thirty-ought-six. "SHE HAD HER TEETH REMOVED, GALLBLADDER REMOVED, RHEUMATIC FEVER, LOST AN EYE, AND . . ."

"SYLVIA!" exclaims her brother. "He didn't ask that! Let me finish!"

"OH, DON'T MIND ME, EVERYONE KNOWS I GOT A STRONG VOICE. SHE HAD NINETY-TWO GRANDCHILDREN AND GREAT, AND GREAT-GREAT. SHE HAD MORE GREAT-GRANDCHILDREN THAN ANYONE . . . FIVE GENERATIONS." Sylvia walks from the kitchen to the bedroom, and then walks back out. I can see her leaning on a table, listening, fidgeting. She can't seem to keep still.

Leonard continues. "Blanche was born in Randolph. May 7, 1897. She married Thomas Jarvis and came here when she was about eighteen. The old stagecoach road went between this house and the barn. The coach had a back rack for baggage

and looked like they do in John Wayne movies. That old route is now just a logging road."

"THAT BIG TREE OUT THERE IS A CAROLINA POPLAR. EIGHTY-EIGHT YEARS OLD, IT'S SIXTEEN YEARS YOUNGER THAN MOM. ROOTS GO UNDER THE HOUSE AND UP TO THE BARN AND DOWN TO THE BROOK 100 YARDS AWAY . . ."

"Sylvia . . ."

"ASH TREE ACROSS THE ROAD GETS JEALOUS A BIT AS WE ALWAYS TALK ABOUT THE POPLAR. IT'S 23 FEET AND 9 INCHES IN CIRCUMFERENCE . . . JUST MEASURED IT. WHEN THE WIND BLOWS THE LEAVES TURN AND IT SOUNDS LIKE RAIN."

"SYLVIA!"

"OKAY. Okay."

"Sylvia," I ask, "why don't you sit down beside your brother and then I can tape both of you?" She has brown hair that hangs straight; she is built squarely, as if her body were formed by hard work, which it was.

"NOPE. JUST AS SOON BE IN THE KITCHEN. YOU CAN HEAR ME OKAY," and she walks back to the kitchen.

"Mom always took care of the sick and dying." Leonard says in his matter-of-fact way. He looks like a kindly neighbor with pink cheeks and silver hair, well fed. "Neighbors used to say, 'You can't die yet as Blanche Jarvis hasn't been here.' For some reason she passed on the comfort people needed when they knew they were going. She and Dad took in quite a few people who were sick, relatives with children, people with mental or physical problems. Relatives

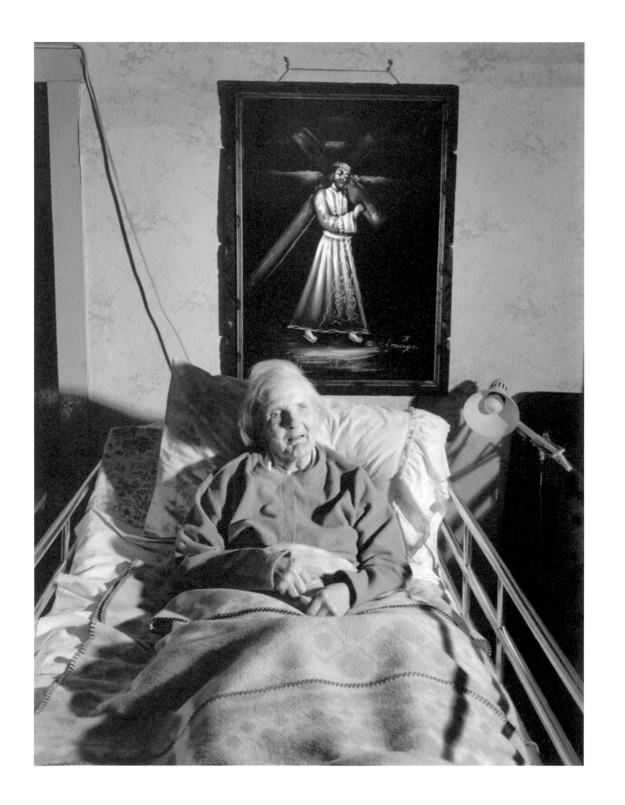

from New Jersey came to live with us during the Depression. No one paid for anything because no one had any money.

"Some came here to live and die. Aunt Gerty and Uncle Ed, Uncle Bill, Granma Bingham — she stayed here twenty-three years and died on her ninety-eighth birthday. Uncle Gary was the only one in the service during World War I. I was twenty-one when I joined the Air Force in World War II. Brother Alfred came up to help run the farm when I was in Africa. I never did come back to farming."

Mom — Blanche — lays on her back, still as an empty room. She had fallen asleep.

"We had cattle, geese, turkeys, chickens, work-horses, and one time we had a herd of sheep and once in a while goats. We separated the cream and butter and fed the hogs the skim milk. Mom used to raid the cream to make strawberry shortcake and Dad would scold her, just for fun. Dad was good with fruit, and we grew apple, pear, and plum trees and we had blueberry, blackberry, and raspberry patches, but we lost the fruit trees in the hurricane of '38."

'WE HAD WILD STRAWBERRIES AND WARM RASPBERRIES OUT OF THE COOKSTOVE."

Leonard is resigned to Sylvia's postscripts. "We'd trade meat and eggs for flour, sugar, and the few things we didn't grow on the farm. Sometimes we paid the taxes with pelts of fox, skunk, wild mink, which was worth a pretty good price, and raccoon and weasels. We had a room upstairs where the furs were stretched inside out on frames."

"MOM LIKED BEST TO BAKE BREAD. WHITE, GRAHAM, AND DARK, SIX LOAVES A DAY. SHE NEVER DROVE A CAR OR HAD A LICENSE. FIRST CAR SHE EVER SAW WAS A MODEL T, I SUSPECT. I COULD HARNESS THE HORSES WHEN I WAS SEVEN."

"Dad had an Overland truck when the Depression came but he put it up and never had a vehicle again."

"MOM MADE CANDY AND SOLD IT TO THE SNOWSVILLE STORE IN EAST BRAIN-TREE. MAPLE CANDY WITH NUTS. BROWN SUGAR CANDY WITH NUTS."

"SYLVIA, let me finish!" I think he is giving up. "My father didn't like to see people go hungry and we always had enough to eat. Why, sometimes we had thirty to forty people for Thanksgiving. Mom would put the extra leaves in the table, and people would sit where they could. Pumpkin pie and English pudding were her favorites, and she made cranberry sauce from dried berries she scooped out of a bin. Mom was either cooking or helping the sick or dying or working in the garden. She never needed more than four hours sleep."

Blanche is awake now, but laying on the bed calm as a still summer evening, seemingly looking out the window at something we can't see. "What is your mother's favorite memory of this farm?" I ask.

Leonard stands up and walks to the bed. He leans over the railing and yells in his mother's ear, "MOM, WHAT WAS YOUR BEST TIME HERE?"

It is an effort but the voice is strong, if gargled. "TH-TH-THANKSVING." She takes a time out and goes at it again. N-N-N CHRISMUS!!!" Her body tenses as she says the phrases, then slumps back on the mattress and her blue eye slips sideways to where I am sitting. She might not hear or talk too well, I think to myself, but her mind is sharp.

Sylvia is at it again. "WE HAD HOMEMADE ICE CREAM, VANILLA, BANANA, AND STRAWBERRY, MADE WITH OUR OWN MILK. I WAS A GOOD MILKER."

"Mom made stuffed turkey and venison for Thanksgiving. Ham and turkey, yams, and sweet potatoes were for Christmas."

"WE HAD COWS NAMED PEARL HARBOR, MAE WEST, SPOTTY, BRINDLE. WE HAD FIF-TEEN COWS, AND WHEN MY HUSBAND CAME WE INCREASED TO TWENTY-FIVE. GOT RID OF THE HORSE AND HAD TRAC-TORS. SOLD THE HERD IN '94. NOW WE CUT HAY FOR OTHER PEOPLE."

"Green beans, yellow beans, squash, Swiss chard, potatoes, canned food, yellow transparents, green rivers, macs, and northern spies, we stored them all in the cellar. Had honeybees too and smoked our own ham with corncobs, and pickled meat and made dandelion wine."

"ONE YEAR SHE BROKE HER LEG IN TWO PLACES, GETTING WOOD IN NOVEMBER. SLIPPED AND FELL, AND THEN SHE GOT DOUBLE PNEUMONIA. SHE WAS IN HER LATE 80s."

"Blanche was brought up by foster parents — the Butterfields — and they never told her that but when she went to school, the kids made fun of her because she was adopted. That hurt her a lot. Later her real parents wanted her back, but her foster parents said they would have to pay for her and they wouldn't pay so they got to keep her."

"SHE WROTE A SONG AND LIBERACE RECORDED IT!"

"NO!" I answer, surprised, or perhaps shocked.

"SHE PLAYED A STEINWAY WITH WOODEN

GRAPES ON IT AND PLAYED THE ORGAN AT SCHOOL."

"Father was Santa Claus."

"SHE WROTE POEMS. LIBERACI RECORDED, *AMERICA OUR OWN*. IT WAS ON A SINGLE 45. MOM WROTE IT WHEN SHE WAS THIRTY-TWO. THE RECORD WAS MADE WHEN SHE WAS SEVENTY-EIGHT."

Then Sylvia sings the song with a beautiful, high sweet voice with perfect pitch, so different from her Yankee cow-calling yell. The song floats through the room and hovers there, faintly, between Blanche and Jesus, before it fades.

America our own, the greatest freest land,
We bow our heads in sacred trust with loyalty we stand.
Our pledge of honesty and truth to thee shall ever be.
We guard each mountain high or low, each plain from
     sea to sea.

The Lessons, thou hast taught of life, live in our heart
     and soul.
To keep thee free from war and strife shall ever be our
     goal.
United all we build our hopes that peace will ever reign.
Our country that's so dear to all, this heritage we claim.

We would that oe'r the entire world, its likeness they
     could keep.
The bloody wars would ever cease, their freedom they
     shall reap.
No ties could ever closer be than this our country's own.
We pray to God you'll ever be, America our own.
America Our Own.

I notice that the tape recorder has stopped working, not that it matters with this interview. I start to take some pictures.

"MOM'S GOT TO LOOK GOOD. DON'T WANT HER DROPPING OFF TO SLEEP.

"MOM! MOM!" and she moves to the back of the bed and leans over the railing, "LOOK! HE'S TAKING PICTURES! LOOK! CLOSE YOUR MOUTH! MOM!"

And she does close her mouth, a bit, and her good eye fixes on me and I know what she is thinking.

On New Year's Eve 2001, Blanche passed away in the Gifford Hospital in Randolph. She so much wanted to be home, but her double pneumonia needed more care than Sylvia could give her. "It just wrenched me," Sylvia told me on the phone, "having her in the hospital, but I was just wore out and she needed care all the time, and oxygen. She was in the hospital for seventeen days and a second pneumonia and congestive heart failure took her."

Blanche had arced through three centuries, living and dying within a few miles of where she was born. She saw relatives or children go to fight in both World Wars, watched the coming of the car and electrification, the downfall of the hillside farm, the destruction of the Trade Towers, and along the way, helped so many people not as fortunate, or as strong, as she.

Anne Lazor — *Yogurt Maker* — Butterworks Farm

Anne Lazor, smooth skinned, relaxed, easy smile, stands on a plateau of perfectly flat land that was famous, at one time, for the amount of rocks that sprouted with every spring plowing. Farmer Trumpass discovered that in 1850 when he first tilled the soil; 125 years later Anne and her husband, Jack, were still harvesting spring rocks when they bought the foundering farm. They were refugees from southern New England who discovered their passion for agriculture while hand milking cows and carrying wooden milk pails at Old Sturbridge Village in Massachusetts. They searched Wisconsin for their ideal farm, found the state wanting, and moved to Vermont, where Jack had lived a year. They bought the Trumpass farm of 60 acres in 1976.

Their dream was a homestead where they would produce their own food.

Within five days of moving in they bought a Jersey cow that produced daily 5 gallons of milk. On a woodstove and gas range in their old kitchen they made cottage and farmer's cheese, butter and yogurt, and bottled raw milk in glass jars. Jack sold the products door to door out of his rusted pickup. He was good at selling.

They increased their cows to six. Jack expanded their markets to stores in nearby towns. Then state inspectors visited. *What are you doing?* they asked. *You can't sell raw milk. You can't process cheese. You can't make yogurt. You need an approved, licensed facility.*

Jack schmoozed them as they built a barn, installed a small plant within it, and constructed an adjoining mill to grind and store their grains. They were quickly approved by the state and named their farm Butterworks. They soon realized that not only

was yogurt the simplest to make of all milk products, it demanded a relatively high price. There are six steps to making yogurt; twice that to produce cottage cheese.

They concentrated on producing three types of yogurt — low fat, vanilla, and lemon. Their herd of Jerseys expanded to forty-five — all from their first cow — increased their acreage to 190, and became organic certified. They grow and mill their own grain to feed the cows and to make bread. The yogurt they make is yellow, creamy smooth in texture, and the closest taste one can find to the tangy,

rich European yogurt. Butterworks now produces 5,000 quarts of yogurt a week that is shipped to stores along the Eastern seaboard. Many of their customers send them fan letters.

"We realized," says Anne, "when we started our farm that food in supermarkets is not what you believe it to be and that you don't know where it comes from or how it is produced. We lost all credibility and trust in the food system. That's why we grow our own produce.

"We make compost and spread it on the fields and have a new greenhouse barn. We keep the earth as fertile and alive as possible, for the more life you have coming up from the ground into the plants and then into the cows makes a healthier herd. They have more ability to resist disease and stress."

Manufactured medicines along with chemical fertilizers are not permitted to be used on the land or animals of an organic farm. If a cow is treated with these products, they must be taken out of production. Anne practices homeopathic medicine, which is compatible with organic farm regulations. It is a skill she learned through work-study groups and her large library, and it has become her passion.

The system of energy-based medicine was formulated by Samuel Hahnemann, a German physician in the early part of the 19th century. Simply put, he believed the cure should be similar to the disease or sickness, that there be one single remedy given in a minimal dose, and that it would be potent. Each medicine is diluted and then shaken, to give it potency. Sometimes the process is repeated thirty times. Nobody knows why shaking the dilution increases the strength.

"Homeopathy is based on physical, mental, and emotional symptoms," says Anne, "and it is pretty hard for a cow to tell you how they're feeling. However, I milk them twice a day and know their personalities. Some are flighty, others may be stubborn, feisty, or placid. If a placid cow is agitated, you know something is wrong. You use your intuition and experience and knowledge of what tincture or pill will work best."

Anne has one cow that comes down with mastitis (inflammation of the udder) every time she leaves the farm for a couple of days. "I know the problem with that cow isn't with mastitis, but with anxiety. I treat it accordingly. Those cows are dependent upon me and perhaps know me better than I realize."

Sometimes, Anne wonders about such dependency. "Is there more to life than milking cows seven days a week, 365 days a year? Am I missing something? I really would like to share what I have learned on this farm with other people, perhaps with people from other countries. And they could teach me."

But for now, she has a herd of Jerseys that depend upon her, day in, day out.

Marjorie Susman and Marian Pollack — *Vegetable Gardeners and Cheese Makers* — ORB WEAVER FARM

More than half of the farm women in this book are *flatlanders* — a Vermont term for those who were not born in the state. Doesn't matter if you have lived in Vermont for half a century, like I have; if you were born out of state you are a flatlander. Sometimes it is said in jest, often not. Yet it is the farming flatlanders, women and men, who have helped sustain and increase the small-farm movement in Vermont, which is now spreading to other states. Their philosophy is to grow and sell regionally — local to local. These farmers have moved to Vermont because the land is less expensive, independence is revered, and agriculture is not as threatened by encroaching suburbia as some other places, although that is changing.

Marjorie Susman and Marian Pollack are outstanding examples of farming flatlanders. In the late 1970s they were living in western Massachusetts where Marjorie studied at the Stockbridge School of Agriculture and worked on a farm. Marian was a family therapist and before that a parole officer in New York City. In Massachusetts they gardened, put up their own food and learned to make a good cheddar in their kitchen. But around them nearby farms went out of business and developments usurped the pastures. As time went on they knew they didn't want to work for other people but produce food for them, and do it in a place removed from suburbia.

Marian: "Let's go be farmers!"

Marjorie: "Neither of us had any money and no family farm either."

Marian: "No trust fund."

Marjorie: "Ziltch."

Marian: "I think that made us efficient farmers."

They answered an ad searching for someone to run a farm in Morrisville, Vermont, and arrived in March 1981. There followed six unhappy months, for neither knew anything about the practical side of farming.

Marian: "I didn't know how to back up the manure spreader with the tractor."

Marjorie: "We didn't know how to turn on the milk pump."

Marian: "We didn't know that water froze."

They learned, in part, from the Lepine sisters, their neighbors who had one of the best Jersey herds in America. Then they answered a wanted ad for help to run a farm in New Haven, Vermont. The farmer who placed the ad had *two* farms: one was where he worked, the other was where he kept his heifers. On the property was a dilapidated barn with

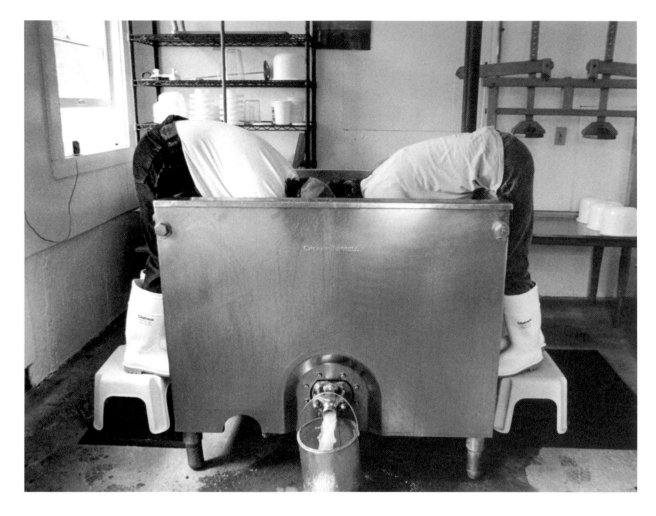

Marjorie: "What we wanted to do when we bought this farm was to make cheese."

Marian: "So in 1995 we sold most of our herd. Kept seven cows to make cheese."

Marjorie: "And we have our garden."

They learned how to keep their organic garden healthy with a mix of green manure, field peas, oats, and other garden waste that they till in. Their garden is on 4 acres, 2 of which remain fallow. They never bought a piece of machinery unless they could pay for it; they still use a push seeder and regard their one helper as much more useful (and pleasant) than a new tractor. They learned not to grow produce that wouldn't sell — a lesson they found out the hard way. One year they planted too many rows of string beans and couldn't sell them at the farmers' market. They came home and ripped out the beans, as it was not worth their while picking them.

Now they concentrate on what sells — ten varieties of lettuce, kale, tomatoes, Swiss chard, red and green peppers, broccoli, leeks, summer squash, zucchini, and onions. They sell to restaurants and a health food store and stopped going to farmers' markets because they had to produce too many varieties of vegetables. They do, however, plant on-order for a few local restaurant chefs.

Their vegetables are certified organic, their cows not.

Marjorie: "The health food store that buys our produce wanted us to be organically certified. Otherwise we wouldn't."

Marian: "People feel the word has been stolen by the government. Trucks now come up here from New Jersey to the store, and their organic produce doesn't always look good. We are looking for another word. I came up with *Verganic*."

They both fret about the ignorance most people have about where food comes from. "Terrorized" is the word they used to describe people's fear of food

no water, no bulk tank, and a gutter cleaner that didn't work. The house hadn't had any love since 1804. The farmer was willing to sell the old farm and take a mortgage, so Marjorie applied for, and won, a grant administered by her old college. (The grant was originally set up by Lotta Crabtree, an actress and dancer who made her fortune in 19th-century saloons in western goldrush towns.)

With the low-interest loan they bought more land and put together a dairy herd of thirty Jersey milkers, including some stock from the Lepines. They fixed up the barn and on a knoll above the house put in a garden with a 180-degree view. The following year they built a cheese house. Marjorie and Marian named their farm Orb Weaver, after that industrious field spider that weaves the big webs. The hard work taught them to be efficient. The low return on their milk taught them frugality. For the next fifteen years they shipped milk, grew vegetables, and made cheese when they could.

Marian: "Once in a while we would make some money."

Marjorie: "We couldn't even breathe, we were working so hard."

Marian: "We lost our focus. We had no time to make cheese."

and why grocery store produce is encased in plastic or pasteurized. One chef who came to their farm was amazed to see lettuce growing.

Marian: "'I thought it came off the back of a truck,' he said."

Marjorie: "It's important to bring good food to the people, so they know what it is. Agritourism will have a future here. They could come to this farm and see a speck of mold on cheese, take it off, and find it is just as good to eat."

Marjorie and Marian work only in the vegetable garden from early summer to fall. Then they make cheese.

Marjorie: "Our cows calve in November, and then we start making cheese. Making cheese in the summer is the most oppressive thing I can think of."

Marian: "When we make cheese we raise the milk to 100°F. Lean over a vat full of hot milk in 95°F weather and you are suffering. The air conditioner doesn't work and waxing cheese is almost physically impossible to do in summer heat."

Marjorie: "Milking in the summer is hot and uncomfortable, for us and the cows. There are flies and bugs."

Marian: "We want to be outside in the summer."

The Orb Weaver dairy herd is pampered with premium hay and are rotationally grazed. They do not feed their cows silage as they believe it makes the cheese bitter. They produce farmhouse cheese they call Colby; some of it is waxed in 2-pound balls. The rest is cured for six months in their new cheese cellar built into a side of a hill and fronted with huge boulders encrusted with fossils. This cheese is dry, with a nutty flavor and very smooth texture, somewhat like Beaufort. It recently won top awards as a farmhouse cheese from the National Cheese Society. They mail order some and sell all they make, mostly to their local customers.

The two Orb Weaver endeavors nicely offset the

precariousness of the weather. During one summer they were hit by a vicious hail storm; it looked like someone went through their garden, shooting holes in their vegetables. Leaves were tattered into confetti. Other times drought turns the soil dry as a two-year-old cow pie. Cheese sales pull them through weather vagaries. A good year and they take the equity and put it into their house, or, as they did recently, buy land. They now have 103 acres.

When Marjorie was diagnosed with breast cancer (she beat it soundly), they took a month off from cheese time and visited Italy. A good garden year recouped their lost income.

Since then, the two farmers have had scheduled leisure time. Every Wednesday afternoon in the summer is free time to read, canoe, or hike. They both are vegetarians and love to cook in their thoughtfully restored farmhouse. They grind their own flour for bread, fire roast chilies to make salsa, and their pizzas are revered.

But they do wonder about the future. The traffic is increasing on their road, and eventually it will be paved. Development may follow.

Marjorie: "Maybe we will sell the farm . . . we can't see the sunset from our farm, and I miss that."

Marian: "I think I would rather not live here while someone else is running the farm. I think the name Orb Weaver will die with us."

Marjorie: "In the meantime it is pretty nice."

Pam Dwyer — *Christmas Tree Farmer* — WILD BRANCH TREE FARM

A December day, cold and clear. The storm that dropped 5 inches of light powder snow before daylight scurried elsewhere. The morning sun arcs low on the horizon, its cold brightness burnishing the new snow. A good day to be alive, or to cut a Christmas tree.

The 20 acres that hold the Fraser firs of the Wild Branch Tree Farm are about 150 yards up a curving trail that passes a machine shed where a group of Vermonters, wool-plaid clad and wearing snow packs, are jawing. The Christmas tree bundler is in front of them, as well as a Kubota tractor. Cars packed with families are pulling into the parking lot. Dad grabs a small saw, and they track the new snow to rows of snow-covered trees. Pam Dwyer walks with them, carrying a broom. She wears a red wool parka and a happy smile that says there's nothing better than to be outside after a new snow when the sun is bright. The trees look like wedding cakes topped with sugar frosting. Pam works her way down the rows and whacks each snow-covered tree with the broom. Plumes of snow sift down. The branches snap up.

Of the 15,000 Christmas tree growers in North America, 350 of them are in Vermont, most of which are choose-and-harvest farms. And of the 35 million trees sold throughout America at Christmas time, the Wild Branch Farm — just a dot in the northern Vermont town of Wolcott — will sell 1,400, give or take.

In 1969 Pam and her husband, Jack, moved on to an old dairy farm drifting into an abyss. The two of them planted Fraser firs in the pastures. Frasers are the third-best-selling species of Christmas tree in America, after balsam and Douglas fir. The Dwyers picked Frasers as they best the sub-zero temperatures their farm endures

"We got 1,000 trees to an acre so we have 20,000," Pam says, as she walks through the rows, whacking trees. For twelve years she was executive director of the Vermont Christmas Tree Association. "If you want to start a Christmas tree farm, be well aware of what you are getting into, which we were not. They need to be planted, weeded, fertilized. Then there's disease and the chance that an early frost damages them. In the summer you prune them so they fill out, since a consumer wants a full tree. After all that you got to sell them. We get $20 for a retail tree, but we also sell a whole bunch at wholesale."

Those are Vermont prices. They go up to $50 in places like New York City. A half century ago there were no Christmas tree farms — the trees were harvested wild. One of the wholesale sellers was Joe Trombley, who lived nearby. He would pay people to cut trees and have them loaded onto freight cars that hauled them as far away as Texas. In the middle of every bundle he hid the "Shirley Temples" — the skinny short trees now known as "Charley Browns."

Joe had his bad moments. In early December 1941, he took a load of Christmas trees to New York City. But after the Japanese attacked Pearl Harbor, he couldn't sell any of them, much less give them away. He had just enough money to get home and buy his children small gifts. It was not that way after 9/11. According to surveys studied by the Christmas Tree Association, there is a trend toward spirituality — people feel threatened by the terrorists and fear an uncertain future. Christmas focuses the family, and the association, of course, believes the best security blanket is a Christmas tree bought from one of their members.

"If you're a Christmas tree farmer," Pam says, "you have to expect ups and down. It could be a recession or it could be a war, or, like it was in the 1950s when the artificial tree came out. That tree was a petroleum product and is not biodegradable and everyone was buying those things. I watched harvesters burn real trees in Morrisville, as they couldn't sell them."

Although Pam complains about the hard work, her favorite time of the year is from October to December — the selling season — when her farm is visited by people who come to cut their own.

"It's funny what turns their fancy. Skinny people will take tall, skinny trees, and big, fat people will pick fat trees. A three- or four-year-old will chose a very small tree. Every time.

"Men are fussier than women. A man wants a dead perfect tree, and a woman is more artistic, and looks at the tree to see how it would look decorated. Oh yes, they have arguments. Most often, they will look at one tree, meander around, and come back to the first one and take that one. I've followed their tracks.

"We work like mad from mid-October until the week before Christmas. Then it is back to normal. Thank God, thank God."

Julie Wolcott — *Sustainable Farmer* — GREEN WIND FARM

Julie Rubaud — *Vegetable Farmer* — ERIC AND JULIE'S PLANTS AND PRODUCE

The winter of 1968: the French ski racer Jean Claude Killy wins three gold medals in the winter Olympics at Grenoble, France, and the Vietnam War is cleaving America. Julie Wolcott, a member of the U.S. National Ski Team, races in Europe on the World circuit. Her specialty is slalom and giant slalom.

"I met her for the first time in 1969," says Gerard Rubaud, a former racer for the French ski team, and at that time Director of Racing for Rossignol Skis. "I was so impressed with the way she was skiing that I had the French ski coach Honoré Bonnet check her out. We agreed she was skiing better than Nancy Greene (World Cup Champion and triple Olympic medalist from Canada) and was as strong if not stronger. Julie would go directly at the gates and at the last moment turn her skis, so she carried her speed for a long time. She skied very much like Killy — very straight up. To do this you need good timing and good muscle quality.

"I so admired Julie that I named my second daughter for her."

In the mid-1970s Gerard, his wife, and two daughters moved to Burlington, Vermont, where he became president of the North American division of Rossignol. In 1983 Gerard resigned and now lives in Westfield, where he bakes bread legendary for its taste and texture, a skill he learned as a child from a farm woman who lived near his family in Aix-les-Bains, France. His elder daughter returned to France, Julie stayed and is now a vegetable farmer. Neither Gerard nor his daughter knew they lived near his daughter's namesake.

It completely blew me away," said Gerard Rubaud, "when I learned, by chance, that Julie Wolcott, who I named my daughter after, was living just a few towns away. It was crazy. For fifteen years we lived that close, and I never knew it. And then, I found, Julie is a farmer and gardener and so is my Julie. I just can't believe it!"

Julie Wolcott, a product of Vermont's junior ski programs, learned to ski and race on small hills near her home in Underhill. Her skill as a junior racer attracted the attention of national coaches and she began training and racing with the U.S. National Ski Team in the late 1960s.

In 1970 Julie was ranked in the top 15 in slalom and giant slalom in the World Cup, but she snuffed her ski career that summer by leaving the team. She refused to wear the U.S. ski team patch and to represent her country.

"There was a bigger picture than what I was doing as a ski racer," remembers Julie, "and it was because of Vietnam. The pressure to be a representative of a national team bothered me. The flag was the issue; it was the symbol of who we are. There is a bigger humanity that we need to represent, and by waving the flag it was singling us out as the best. It is not part of global understanding. I think we have lost our humanity as a nation, where things have become more important than people. I felt that my racing wasn't for the betterment of the world."

"What could you do for the betterment of the world?" I ask. It was late fall. There was a nip in the

air when the sun settled into the horizon. Farmers were spreading manure on their fields before the first snow. Julie's partner, Stephen, was replacing the siding on the front of their barn. The decision she made thirty-one years ago directed her to this farm on a dirt road little traveled in Fairfield, Vermont.

"I could garden," she said, almost in a whisper.

After resigning from the U.S. ski team, Julie briefly attended Stamford University in California before she returned to Stowe, Vermont, and worked as a ski coach and baked bread in a health food store. "I learned that I didn't want to please people for business reasons. It was hard to be good enough for our customers. The bread didn't rise enough . . ." In the early '70s Vermont was in metamorphosis. Underhill, located in an agricultural valley on the other side of Stowe and Julie's home, was repositioning itself as suburbia. Julie didn't wish to live in that culture or in the ski and tourist frenzy of Stowe.

In 1977 she went to live with Stephen, a friend who was maple sugaring in Fairfield. Fairfield was an area she first discovered on a bicycle when she was sixteen. Only 25 miles from her childhood home, it is bereft of large mountains and recreational tourism; there is little more than farms, and rolling, twisting gravel roads. Julie settled in, planted an organic garden, and never left.

Julie and Stephen now live on a family farm that they slowly expanded from nine horses and five goats on 50 acres to twenty-five Jersey cows, two workhorses, and a 3,700-tap sugarbush on 200-plus acres. She and Stephen share the chores of milking

and producing the 700 gallons of syrup. Julie maintains a pick-your-own strawberry garden, and her vegetable garden feeds the family. They heat their home with wood cut on their property. They have no television and only now are they considering linking up to the Internet ("I am being pressured," says Julie). Two of their children have graduated from college, two are in the local schools.

Julie looks very much as she did when she was racing: thin but strong, delicate bone structure, eyes that penetrate with an almost mystical light. Her hair is threaded into a thin pony tail. She is soft spoken to the point of a whisper.

"Our farm has given our kids a visible, concrete purpose. They know why they are doing the chores, they see the end result. It gives structure to their day.

"But I question myself. Is this life adequate for my kids? Is it what they need? Will they be healthy individuals and citizens? Should we have television? Are they culturally exposed to enough diversity? Would they reach their potential given the base we offered

them? It seems that they have, and now it is up to them."

"She is the most spiritual woman I know," one of Julie's friends told me. Perhaps she is more of a philosopher and construes a practical life from abstracts. She recalls the act of ski racing:

"There is an effortless freedom to skiing. Slalom poles on a hill are precise points, and I had to figure out how to ski efficiently and fluidly around those points with the least amount of motion. At one time ski racing was the medium of my life. Now there are other mediums where I still exercise those same kinds of decisions. Perhaps skiing and my life as I live it are not so far apart."

Every other year Julie skis for a day at nearby Jay Peak, which annually offers a free day pass for a Vermont farmer. One year Julie goes. The next year Stephen goes, but together they spend a lot more time on their snowshoes in the sugarbush.

Things were going smoothly for Julie Rubaud. A bright woman with an academic bent, she was a senior majoring in English and philosophy at the University of Vermont and had won a scholarship to attend graduate school at the University of Montreal.

"I woke up one morning — I was at school, in my last year of college, in 1992 — and said to myself

that I was going to farm. Don't ask me why; I think farming chose me. I would be miserable doing anything else."

For the next eight years Julie worked at Intervale, a communal garden complex in Burlington. It was there she met Eric, who became her partner in life and vegetables. There they honed their skills and developed markets for their produce.

For five years they searched for land to buy when a friend told them of 350 acres in Starksboro that was being sold by a land trust. Unfortunately, it was too large and costly for them until a buyer from Arizona called and said they wanted to purchase over half of it for beef cattle. They had seen the land on the Web from U.S. Government Survey Photos and . . . "They were Santa Claus" said Julie "Just everything came together with this farm." They bought the property in 2000 and named their farm Eric and Julie's Plants and Produce.

Of the 108 acres they purchased, 70 are tillable and 30 of those are planted in organically grown cash crops. They built a unique barn. Downstairs is a cement floor with a loading dock and a cold storage room. Tractors can drive in and out of the barn, and they have enough storage space for equipment. Upstairs live Julie, Eric, and their five-year-old daughter, Louissa.

On the farm they grow all types of vegetables, herbs, edible blossoms, and flowering vines, but their specialty are dozens of varieties of salad greens. They deliver to stores and nurseries and sell at farmers' markets. In 2002 they established themselves as a community subscribed farm and have 250 members, who, during the season, pick up their vegetables at the farm every week.

Julie has inherited the French trait of using the best ingredients in what you eat.

"Kids love good food. My dad is always saying he would never consider making food that kids don't like. They eat his bread and never want to eat any other bread again. Kids who won't touch a vegetable will take a pea off the vine and it's like candy to them, but they won't touch a frozen pea. I love to have them come to the farm and just run around and have fun and see where their food is grown.

"People don't connect their food with the earth. Our nutrition comes from the soil, the vegetables are synthesizing the nutrients that are in the ground into the form we can assimilate, but our soils all over the country are being completely trashed by chemicals. Artificial nutrients are being pumped in so our nutrition bank is being completely eroded. What I am saying is that many of the products we buy off shelves have nutrients in them from a chemical added to the soil. No longer is it coming out of the living soil."

Julie's biggest surprise, as a Vermont farmer, has been to find that her namesake was also a farmer and gardener. Gerard Rubaud was delivering bread to a store, and Julie Wolcott's sister worked there. The conversation got around to skiing and to Julie Wolcott. Gerard was flabbergasted to find that his daughter's namesake is a gardener, as his daughter is, and his family lived within miles of Julie Wolcott.

"It was mind blowing to find this out," says Julie Rubaud, who was born in Mégève, France, in 1971, the year Julie Wolcott quit the U.S. ski team. "I had spoken to her a number of times over the phone about organic fertilizer deliveries but didn't know who she was. We met at my dad's house and visited their farm, and it is so beautiful. It says a lot about the love and consciousness they have in their work.

"Julie's a mentor to me, as she has been farming so long and impressively and has remained small. She doesn't blow her horn. She worked hard with their local school to have agriculture included as part of the curriculum on a daily basis and helped the school establish a garden. She persuaded the school to accept locally grown produce in their cafeteria. She did this by herself, while most people do it with grants and institutional support. She is a mentor to people who come to her for advice on educating schoolchildren about agriculture."

The real wonder, of course, is how the two Julies, linked by first names, born thousands of miles apart and in different countries, growing up speaking different languages, could end up living so close to each other and share similar philosophies, both working the soil. Is it a coincidence? Or . . .

Amy Pomeroy and Yukiko Washizu — *Dairy Farmers and Cheese Makers* — POMEROY FARM

Summer of 1999. A day of clarity, hot but not sticky — perfect weather to rake fresh-cut hay. Amy Pomeroy is the most relaxed of tractor operators — her feet are up on the cowling and she leans back, as though sun bathing on the beach, and steers with one hand. On the straightaway she gives a nudge, now and then, to the wheel. She makes smaller and smaller squares — past the old tree-lined cemetery, stone-walled from the field to protect the twenty-five tombstones of farm families who died more than 150 years ago. On the other side of the field she rakes past an empty tennis court, and a dust cloud of hay chaff swirls behind the tractor.

Middletown Farm is owned by Barbara and Wendy Rowland and would be called a gentleman's farm except Jesse Pomeroy rents it — the barn, pastures, fields — all he owns are the cows, the equipment, and his debt. He even rents hay fields from other people. In this year forty cows are milked, hardly enough to sustain a one-income farm. Only two dairy farms in Londonderry and South Londonderry remain operating.

Amy, twenty-one, is the daughter of Jesse. She has just graduated from Agricultural School at SUNY Cobleskill, where she concentrated on dairy farming. For a twenty-one-year-old she knows her way around a hay field and a milking parlor. Jesse watches from a corner of the field as his daughter rakes the hay that he will soon bale and talks about the art of operating a tractor.

"You got to be born to be good at it, to drive a tractor. I think I was a natural but, well . . . I started when I was five years old. The ones who have an interest in starting young are the naturals. Our son didn't like it but . . . you take Amy out there. You can look at a person on a tractor for a couple of hours and you can tell whether they are a natural. Amy's got it. She was good with equipment even before she wanted to farm. If you operate farm equipment right it doesn't need to be maintained so often."

Amy has turned over the controls of the tractor to a friend, Jennifer Cobb, who is learning to work part

time on the farm. Amy stands behind her and directs her to make even lines of raked hay so it's easy for the baler to suck up.

"When I was a young man," Jesse's accent sounds like it is rooted in Oklahoma, "I was a lot harder on the equipment than Amy is. Women have a gentler touch and they make a lot better milkers. Amy calls the cows by name and strokes them.

"I'm happy to have women working here, as I think they do a better job with a lot of things, and with the new equipment they don't need the brute strength that sometimes a woman doesn't have." Amy and Jesse have a rapport that is more like friends than father and daughter.

On the barn and in the milk house are number of signs. *Don't complain about farmers with your mouth full; Drinking milk is legal at any age. Run with the best, John Deere; What do you call a cow that doesn't give any milk? An udder failure.*

Barbara Rogers is cleaning out the cow stalls. She works barefoot in the summertime.

Amy is sucking a lollipop as she controls the milking machines. As she finishes up and goes outside to stand in the brightness of the setting sun, she talks about herself. She coaches basketball, works with 4-H kids, and teaches Sunday School.

"I like milking, and haying is fun. You get used to working seven days, but my dad and I spell each other so we have a couple of days off. It is hard to make a living milking only forty cows. If we made cheese we would downsize our operation. We looked into bottling our own milk, but there are so many regulations we decided cheese is the better way to go."

Summer of 2002. Jesse is remarried and his new wife, Marian, is in charge of cheese making. Walled off from the cluttered office and milking parlor that is continually hosed down of manure and urine is a new cheese-processing room where the equipment is aluminum, clean, and sparkling. They produce Jesse's Middletown Cheese, an aged, English-style cow's milk cheese of their own recipe and are setting up a distributorship.

Amy no longer works at the farm. She had some back problems, and, as she knows so well, "The farm cannot support two families." She now works with a veterinarian and finds she has a skill there, particularly with large animals. She does artificial insemination for her father's herd. Amy will soon be married and plans to have a few beef cattle at her new home.

Jennifer Cobb, the tractor trainee, is now working as a landscaper. Barbara, the barefoot barn cleaner, has left but Jesse still has the knack to find farm women. The new milker is Yukiko Washizu, who grew up just south of Tokyo, Japan. Always smiling, she handles the six-stall milking parlor with quick efficiency, never hurrying but always moving, a trait of an efficient farmer.

Yukiko wanted to see the United States and enrolled in Green Mountain College in Poultney. A professor interested her in agriculture, and she finished a two-year course in gardening. There she met her husband, who was also in agriculture studies and is now at McGill studying religion. He plans to be a teacher.

Yukiko milks twenty-eight cows, twelve less than Amy did. "We keep more cows than we need for making cheese," says Marian, Jesse's wife, "because we need the fertilizer for the fields. Good manure makes good hay — and that makes good farmstead cheese." The milk they do not use for cheese is shipped to Agri-Mark, the Vermont co-op.

"I love farming," says Yukiko. "No, I had never been on a farm until I came to Vermont. I want to have my own someday, with cows and sheep and goats and pigs — a small farm — Yes!" and she flashes a bright smile. "My husband will be a teacher and I will do the farming. I would like to farm in Vermont, maybe in the western part of the state. Pawlet, or Rupert. It is warmer and has a longer growing season."

Yukiko, for now, waits for her husband to finish his graduate studies. She does some baby-sitting and makes soap out of vegetable oil and milk and sells it at the local farmers' market along with Jesse's Middletown Cheese made from the cows she milks.

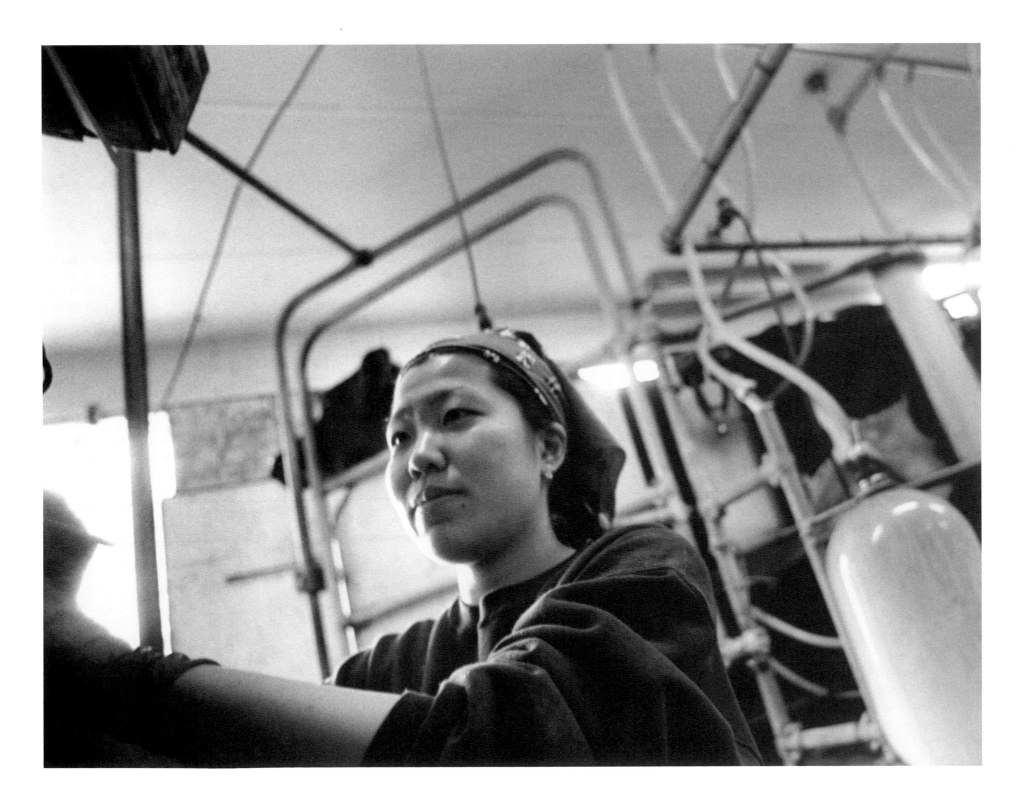

Amanda Ellis-Thurber — *Vegetable and Flower Gardener* — LILAC RIDGE FARM

"Love at first sight," is what Amanda calls it when she met Ross Thurber. They were agricultural students at the University of Vermont. Ross asked her down to Brattleboro to visit the family farm and took her on the upper road that slices through two hay fields and has an expansive view of the property. It was December 23, 1995, a keenly bright day of winter sun and fresh snow that was lightly sifted on the fields. Ross led Amanda up to a 100-year-old oak. From its base they looked out on an180-degree view.

"I came into myself that day," remembers Amanda. "I knew this was home — just knew it. I think I was displaced where I grew up, in Cleveland, like a pickle in a suburban landscape. This place is magical."

Amanda and Ross were married the next year. Red haired, ambitious, a Scorpio in passion, energy and direction, at the age of six Amanda became interested in agricultural history, and in college she immersed herself in studying the conversion of farms to organic practices and in farms bent by cultural and economic changes.

Before her marriage she was a hired hand on Lilac Ridge Farm, as the Thurbers call their spread. She milked, logged, and maple sugared. She also planted a small vegetable and flower garden before her marriage to Ross for use at home and for the wedding, but she quickly expanded it. She had book learning — her degree is in horticulture — but mostly she learned how to garden by the seat of her pants.

"I'm intuitive about gardens. It's my style, to shoot from the hip. Oh, I can be erratic but it works out. I love being with living things. I love working outside and feeding people and the community, and I like doing it in a way that's good for the soil."

She grows vegetables and flowers organically, although, like most small and commercial farm gardens in Vermont, hers is not certified.

Certified or not, her practices and her intuition proved to be working. Within five years her garden was netting $20,000 a year and had grown to the second biggest income maker for the farm, after milk from their Holstein–Brown Swiss herd, and ahead of maple syrup, logging, and Christmas trees. Much of her success can be attributed to their location — six miles from Brattleboro, which has a robust farmers' market. There are many local restaurants and stores that buy their produce. They sell everything they grow.

The Thurber farm is a partnership. The income goes in a pot, and each family member has a draw for basic living expenses. At the end of the year they look at their statements and usually, if there is a profit, they reinvest it in the farm. Their expenses are low, as they live on the farm, which has been in the family for two hundred years.

Stuart, Ross's father, was one of the first to realize the importance of preserving farmland not only for themselves but for the good of the community. In the 1970s a developer planned to convert the land near the Thurbers into condominiums and a golf course. The Brattleboro town manager knew that development escalates the cost of infrastructure and taxes. Together with local farmers, Stuart and the town organized to save the land for agriculture.

Now the Thurber farm has expanded to 600 acres, most all of it conserved for agricultural use. The farm can presently support two families. "Our idea is not to create a monster of a farm but to be better at what we do," says Ross. "Farmland developed into lots is not an attractive idea," adds Stuart.

Ross works with Stuart on the dairy operation, but slowly the responsibilities are switching to the younger Thurber. Well, sort of. The farm can't make due without Beverley, Stuart's wife, and Amanda knows this.

"Beverley pays the bills and the taxes. She is not driven by her agenda and will drop anything to help out. She knows how to milk, bale hay, wrap the round bales, wash out the milk house, and pick greens. She helps me at the farmers' market on Saturday, and she sells at the Wednesday market. She does milk testing, and the Christmas trees are her project; she keeps them trimmed and well shaped and sells them every Christmas season."

Amanda hesitates a bit, then smiles, more at herself. She is a strong-willed woman who is learning from a quiet mentor.

"Beverley is the guru that holds us together; the rest of us are just playing in the sandbox."

Ruth Shumway — *Dairy Farmer* — GREEN ACRES MILKING SHORTHORNS

The end of the 20th century was not good to Ruth Shumway. One of four children, she took over Green Acres, the family farm in North Hartland that had been bought by her grandfather in 1910. Located on the rich river-bottom soil next to the Connecticut River, it was a classic. The round barn was a Vermont icon, and their home was protected by two huge black walnut trees, probably planted in the 1800s when the house was built. One tree was knocked down by a hurricane in the early 20th century, the other still stands and is a landmark. Ruth and her first husband, Russ Demmon, had a herd of Holsteins and Milking Shorthorns, a strawberry roan breed brought into this country from England in 1783.

In 1971 her husband divorced her. Three years later the beautiful round barn burned down — the victim of children playing with matches — and thirty head of cattle were destroyed. Ruth remarried in 1977 but four and a half months later her husband, Bud Shumway, was killed when a ditch he was digging caved in. A 1989 midnight fire destroyed her farmhouse and another house next to it; they were lucky to get out alive. The huge black walnut tree was all that was left standing.

"Well, that was that," says Ruth. "Running that farm by myself was just too much. My daughter lived in Bethel, so I decided to buy a farm near her."

Like many small farmers, Ruth considers herself a caretaker of the land and animals she is entrusted with, so she left a legacy to protect Green Acres. "I didn't want houses built on the family farm," she said. "The Upper Valley Land Trust bought the acreage next to the river, and then I gave them some woodland, altogether about 300 acres. The

stipulation is that it can only be used as farmland. I owned a couple of islands — about 17 acres — in the Connecticut River, and I donated that to the Nature Conservancy as some rare plants grow there.

"And when I sold my home, I made provisions for that remaining huge black walnut. It's the largest in Vermont and some say in the country — 16 feet in circumference. I didn't want it taken down for lumber. If something happens to the tree, the land trust takes 40 percent of the proceeds, 40 percent

goes to the local fire department and 10 percent each to the local church and the humane society."

In January of 1993 Ruth moved herself and eighty head of Shorthorns to her new farm in East Randolph. It is a compact farm of 96 acres stretched into a narrow valley. "I've been farming for fifty-eight years and the first couple of years here were rough, trying to make ends meet. I was doing it all by myself, milking forty-eight head. On the other farm we had two hundred head and hired help.

"I'm not getting any younger and my shoulder is gone. I went to the doctor and he X-rayed it and said my rotator cuff was gone. They didn't know where it went. I guess I rotated it too many times. For years I carried 1,000 pounds of milk a day that had to be dumped into a center station in the old barn in Hartland.

"So I had an operation. Doesn't hurt so much, but the arm isn't much good for anything. My other shoulder hurts, and my knees are going. Now my back is bothering me. This is the way it is with older farmers."

Relatives help out. A nephew and his wife live in an apartment in her house, and work part time, as do two women who come in for the morning milking. Her granddaughter Kylie is now in agriculture school and is the designated heir. In a year she will have finished college and will return to the farm.

"I've made arrangements for her to take over the farm, but I will remain and work with her," said Ruth.

When Ruth left Hartland, she gathered nuts from the surviving old black walnut that had become a symbol of the years her family farmed Green Acres. The tree weathered births, deaths, divorces, and fire; just as Ruth did. She's planted more than thirty black walnuts around her house in South Royalton. One is 25 feet tall.

Deb Ravenelle — *Logger* — Sterling Mountain Farm

Since the days of its settlers, rural Vermont has been divided into two cultural camps: hill people and valley people. The first valley people settled Vermont's villages, and they remain there today. They need neighbors for gossiping, their houses are painted white, and their lawns are neatly mowed. They are the town clerks, store and hotel owners, bankers, blacksmiths, carpenters, small manufacturers, widows, lawyers, and real estate agents. Valley people are more political than hill people and do not give too much thought to seeing the sun rise or set.

Those who settled the hills were loggers, farmers, trappers, and hunters. They were the more adventurous of the first settlers, clearing pastures near mountaintops and plowing for their foundation stones. The land was inexpensive, neighbors were sparse, and the remoteness strengthened independence and freedom. "I come from Vermont; I do what I want" was and is the mantra of the hill people. They often situated their homes so they were the first to see the sunrise or the last to see the sunset.

Deb Ravenelle is a hill person. She moved to Vermont from Connecticut to learn agriculture and forestry at Sterling College. When she finished college she settled on a dead-end road in Montgomery, near the Canadian border.

Red hair (usually in a pigtail), a fine bone structure, a sharp frown if she doesn't know you too well, and a bursting, often self-deprecating, laugh; these are her features. Deb always liked horses, but in Vermont she fell in love with workhorses — Belgians, to be specific. This is how she describes her love for the woods and horses:

It was second grade for me, growing up in the suburbs of Connecticut. I can remember the teacher asking all of the students in the class what they wanted to be when they grew up. When it came my turn to bear my soul, I said, "I want to make a living with the land."

Michael Orr, my bright, red-haired classmate, with a face filled with freckles, blurted out, "You can't do that anymore."

The entire class roared with laughter — and my face turned as crimson as Michael Orr's hair.

And here I am, some thirty-odd years later, having made a living most of my adult life with this sweet Mother Earth.

Some things in one's life never change. I grew up with woods outside our house. I loved going into the woods to explore, play Daniel Boone, hike to the caves. I also always had such a strong attraction to horses. Why? Who knows . . . but I've always believed in doing the

things we are drawn to do — and to live inside our dreams. What else is there?

One of two loves of my life has been to be in the woods — and this has evolved into working with horses.

When I first became acquainted with Rob, my sweetheart (I was traveling to Alaska to look for work on a fishing boat; he was taking a break from Vermont), he asked me: "So, I just don't get it, what is it about women and horses?"

That's not a question I have an easy answer to. For me, horses are just such beautiful animals to look at and be around. They represent a deep sense of freedom, even though they require a commitment of so much care. And when you have a horse and work with it every day, you develop a wonderful relationship of trust and affection for one another.

When I bought my horse Champ, a Belgian gelding, from a man in his early fifties, I did a classic foot-in-your-mouth. As I handed him a check to pay for Champ, I said, "Oh, it must be nice to get a little cash in your pocket."

I looked, as I loaded the horse in my trailer, and saw big tears welling up in his eyes. He had watched Champ be born some nine years earlier and had certainly grown attached to this horse. As the years went on, I distinctly understand the affection this man could have for this particular horse.

When I bought Champ, he was a handful. A big, healthy horse, a little hot at times, brimming with energy. Champ had a very big heart, he worked hard, always giving the job at hand his best.

Whenever I went into the pasture and Champ saw

me, he would come to visit. It wasn't for apples — although I occasionally would have one — it was for hugs. He would take his big head and wrap it around my back and pull me gently into him. I have never seen any other horse who loved a hug so much. It became a daily routine for us.

Once, when I was boarding my horses close to a job, I arrived in the morning to find two young children in his pasture. Champ was reaching his big long neck down to say hello to them. He somehow understood when to be very gentle around children or feeble adults.

Another morning, as I arrived on my log job, my horses were laying down and resting. I woke them and they stood up. I was scratching Champ's neck, he was nuzzling Paul's back, and I was squished between the two. I said out loud, "Jeeze, Champ, do you think we can get any closer?" They then had breakfast. I sharpened my saws, and we went to the woods. It was a wonderful, cool early summer day. We pulled out the first hitch of the day, the top part of a pine tree. When you work a team, you become one — like a Zen experience, you understand each other's moves — two horses, one human, moving in unison, like one being combined. You move forward together, you move backward together . . . you back onto a hitch. It becomes a flow of energy, a flow of work together. It feels really good.

The second hitch of the day was a bigger hitch. We backed onto it, hitched up, and headed to the landing. We stopped to rest before going up a short hill. Then started again. All of a sudden, Champ looked off. We stopped at the top of the hill and he couldn't relax, wanted to keep moving. We moved again and he started swaying and then fell down.

I unhitched Paul and tried to get Champ up — he couldn't. I ran down to the landowner's house, called the vet and Rob, and ran back into the woods. By the time the vet and Rob arrived, Champ was dead. I was on top of his big body, bawling like a two-year-old. Champ had just had his twentieth birthday. Rob and I had just closed on buying the sugarbush of our dreams two days before.

Why now, Champ? I want to build you my dream barn and let you retire there. Champ had one big heart attack and was gone.

Another answer to Rob's question — I loved that Champ horse with all my heart. I had worked with him on log jobs all over northern Vermont, and I longed to bring him home onto our own land and work with him there. But, I guess with Champ passing at that point in my life, I'm reminded (and need reminding) that life is not about getting there . . . life is about the journey there. And I definitely so much enjoyed my journey through time with Champ . . . as I now do with Paul and Burt.

Horses continue to inspire me. I hope to live like Champ — to live life to its fullest until it is time to pass on — to live in the dream . . .

During the summer of 2001, two years after Champ died and their purchase of a 206-acre woodlot and sugarbush, Deb used Paul and Burt (he's the one who likes to stick his tongue out) and her chain saw to cut and drag out hemlock, spruce, pine, and tamarack. A portable sawmill turned the logs into lumber from which they built a hay barn. Then she and Rob cleared a pasture and a house and barn site. The home site is on a hill and faces a sterling panoramic view of mountain ridges and basins.

At night you can't see a light from a house or a car, just stars touching the mountain ridge.

Construction costs for a new house are beyond the couple; maple syrup income is not enough, and Rob has been footing any extra expenses from a sports store he owns. Deb plans to increase her share with a new business she calls Sterling Mountain Logging. She is hiring herself out to do horse logging, timber-stand improvement, house-site clearing, and small woodlot management. And she lives near Stowe, where she and her Belgians chauffeur wedding guests from here to there in a fancy wagon.

In the future they hope to expand the sugarbush so that it will pay the mortgage and the property taxes on their 206-acre farm. "At least, that's what we hope to do within the next fifteen years," says Deb.

In the meantime she expects to be known as the horse logger and maple sugarer, and to always lack enough tubing so that she and Paul and Bert can climb the mountain to those trees hung with buckets and bring the sap down to the sugarhouse, where Rob is boiling.

Ellen H. Hamilton — *Retired Farmer's Wife* — Sunny Hill Farm

She was born Ellen Howe in 1922, one of nine children, and was brought up on one of three Howe farms in Tunbridge. She married a farmer, Joe Hamilton, and moved to his farm in West Brattleboro where she raised seven children. A few of her memories of her life on the farm, as a child, and as a mother:

"We learned to work. Didn't matter whether you were a boy or girl, there were chores to do and no question about that. It was our way of living.

"We were a dairy farm, and my father also peddled fresh meat and sometimes vegetables. We never had heard of a freezer. We filled the wood box, picked up eggs, weeded the garden, and picked the produce. During the school year we made the beds and put things in order so Mother could get on with the day's work. It was quite an assignment for the nine of us.

"In the summer I raked the hay away from the fences. Every spear. And I had to ride the workhorse when cultivating the corn. It was the worst job and I was always sore from riding, but if I walked I was afraid I would be tread on.

"When everyone had mumps I volunteered to feed the calves and ever after that was my job. I didn't mind it. Another job was to pitch down the silage. In the winter it was frozen and that was a devil. I won't forget it. I had the feeling my father didn't want girls. They cost money, I suppose, and boys could do more work, but we did pretty well.

"Elementary school was one mile and a half away, and we walked. One day it was so cold you could only see our eyes through our scarves. We couldn't leave our faces exposed without getting frozen. There was a gang of us that walked, maybe ten kids at a time.

"We did sliding in the winter on the hills behind the farm. We would take the travois sled down at a pretty good clip. It had two runners in front and two runners in back. Up front one of us steered and in the back another worked the brake. Four of us in between hung on and screamed. Once during the full moon it was icy and we went over a ski jump my brothers built. Lucky some of us weren't killed.

"It was the best thing in life living on the farm — it was the closeness of the family. We didn't have TV or cars and we played games and on weekends made popcorn and fudge. We had the river to swim in. Mother always had strawberry shortcake on the table when we came home from Bible School.

"I met Joe when he came to visit our farm in Tunbridge. Well, I already had a friend but it worked out, didn't it? I went to college and then to secretarial school. I was working in Springfield, and one fall weekend I visited my sister on their farm in West Brattleboro and Joe came to visit from his farm. It was after milking and dark and he walked over Round Mountain to see me — about 4 miles. He told me he found his way by keeping the North Star to his back. Seems as though he just got here when he had to go back, for he had early milking to do. It was much too short. Then he walked home, but this time followed the road, which was an 8-mile trip. Stupid. It was during the war and there was gas rationing, but he didn't have a car anyhow.

"Well, of course we got married; we were in love. I sewed my own wedding gown and everything else. I wasn't going to ask Dad to do that . . . you aren't kidding I was independent

"We moved into the Hamilton farm with no elec-

tricity, but who cared? But it was darn nice when we got it. In the house was Joe's mother and grandfather and a feeble-minded uncle. It was crowded, but that's the way it was.

"There wasn't much difference between the way I and my children were brought up. Everyone had chores. I had to keep the food coming, the clothes washed, clean house, tend the vegetable garden, and put up about five hundred jars of food in the fall. We didn't take many trips to the grocery store. We had to transfer the milk every day down to the main road, and we used a sled to take the manure out of the barn. The greatest invention of the time was the gutter cleaner, and after that was the silo loader. Five of my children live within 5 miles, but none of them farm.

"I liked sugaring. Everyone did. I canned the syrup and made sure the strainers were clean and sometimes lugged wood and supplied the doughnuts. We had sugar on snow at home on the dining table. I set individual bowls of snow on the table, as I liked to pour my own syrup so it didn't get stuck together."

When her son Kevin took over the family farm, Joe and Ellen moved into a small house they built a few hundred yards up the road. Ellen came with her Home Comfort wood cookstove that she wouldn't give up, although she also has an electric oven. "Pies taste better when they come out of a woodstove," she says. Their house is heated with a wood furnace. She still plays the organ for the church and has a piano at home. On the day I was there she was canning peaches. One jar didn't seal up right so she opened it and served peach cobbler for lunch.

Betty Foster — *Widow* — Foster Farm

Mimi Neff — *Artificial Inseminator* — Little Holden Farm

When Charley Foster dropped dead on the linoleum floor in the dimly lit kitchen of the family farmhouse, the farm died with him. Family farms are just that — they depend upon family to do the work. If there is no one to fill in or carry on, the farm will die.

Foster Farm lies on the downside of a plateau overlooking a glorious view of the Green Mountains, from Terrible Mountain in Weston south to Magic Mountain. The hay fields slope gently to the barn and farmhouse and then flow toward the valley. A central chimney delineates the classic proportions of the house, weather-seared outside and aged on the inside by a century and half of use. Family photos and paintings of the farm, done by neighbors, hang on the wall of the living room. Plaster figurines of cows stand on shelves. An old television, a low bookshelf, a rocking chair, a couch, and a heater fill the floor space. In the kitchen where Charley died the woodwork is painted green with old gray paint peering through in patches. There are layers upon layers of wallpaper, dully varnished by woodstove cooking and oil lamps, aged by generations of families and the hired hands who lived here.

The fields that surround the house are bereft of the Holsteins Charley used to milk. If the hay fields are not mowed, in a dozen years they will grow into scrub brush. Without the heat of livestock, a few harsh winters will crumble the barn's ridgeline. The hay wagons are falling apart, and hay is rotting in the bed, although the tractors look serviceable even though they are rusted.

Charley knew, two years before he died, that the farm was on borrowed time. He was diagnosed with farmer's lung and told to stay out of the barn, so he sold his milkers. His next door neighbor, Mimi Neff, kept fifteen cows in his barn and worked her herd up to forty by the time Charley died. They too were dispersed. Betty Foster, his widow, still lives in the house. Their son and his family occupy an attached apartment, although he never had interest in farming.

Charley's death was also the death of dairy farming in Weston, for his was the last working dairy farm. Most of the other farm homes have been renovated and occupied by a wealthier group of people. With his passing Betty Foster will wait out the last years of her life, and Mimi Neff, well, part of her life died too.

Mimi and her husband, Perry, live in a comparatively new house, impeccably landscaped with a small red barn. It is just yards down the road from Foster Farm. The house is filled with early-American antiques, paintings, and a fine old grandfather's clock. Perry Neff was a banker with the Chemical Bank in New York until he retired and moved with Mimi to Vermont. Although most of her life was spent in Long Island, Mimi summered in Vermont as a young girl and learned to milk cows by hand. Ever since, cows were important to her, so when they moved here, in 1973, it was only natural for the Fosters to become close friends.

Charley's bible was a book on breeding, and his hobby and business was improving his Holstein herd. He kept wonderful records, and Mimi was intrigued. Eventually, Charley took Mimi to a consignment auction in New Hampshire, and she bought her first cow. Through the years, Mimi had learned from Charley that there wasn't enough genetic diversity in the local bulls, so she took a ten day artificial insemination course that offered field experience breeding cows in a slaughterhouse.

Soon Mimi was ordering semen from the top Holstein bulls in America, and within eight years the Foster herd's production of milk went up. Mimi was breeding cows throughout the region, and she became president of the local chapter of the American Holstein Association.

"I spent as much time in Charley and Betty's house as I did in my own. It was the worst year of my life when he died and the beginning of the end of the farm," says Mimi. "Even today when I pass that barn, I cry. I was breeding five hundred cows a year in the late 1980s. Now I'm down to just a few."

It is an April day of brilliant sun bouncing off snow several feet deep, the light sharp as a knife point. It has been a heavy and long winter. In the parlor it is warm, and morning light flows through the windows.

Betty Foster sits in the center of the couch, her hands clasped together. She sits silently, as if she too were a framed photo on the wall. Alzheimer's is seeping into her brain and has wiped out the dates in her life — the year she was married, the year Charley died.

I break the silence and ask Betty about specific

blueberries that grew along the edges of the fields. On hot summer days she liked to walk up to the spring that was tiled and surrounded by violets and lady's-slippers. There was a glass mug stuck upside down on a stick that she would submerge in the well and fill with icy water, so cool and refreshing. The view from the upper fields was of blue-hazed mountains, patches of hay bending in the northwest wind, and green pastures. There was always a breeze pushing the clouds to the other side of the valley — this she remembers best. There were no houses in this view of fields and mountains, save their own.

When I mentioned how her sister-in-law, Dottie, describes the spring, she breaks into the silence.

"Isn't it pretty up back there? I love the mountains."

She sits for a while longer, and then continues.

"Newcomers, moved here and never said hello. Then they moved out. I guess they didn't want to be bothered with poor people. We used to count on our neighbors."

"See that house on Terrible Mountain?" It is a white house sticking out like a boil on the mountainside. I mention the name of the owner. "It ruins the beauty of my mountains . . . he's not my type."

We talk about real-estate development and a relative of hers that is a developer.

"I disowned him."

Silence returns and we sit here, as if meditating. She hasn't moved.

"God I would like to see some green," Betty says. The room was almost incandescent with sun-suffused light surrounding Betty. Her memory is like a database being erased bit by bit but the fragments keep coming out, snippets of her life. Perhaps she is thinking of Charley and the way he died when she says, "The only way I will leave this place is feet first."

But she didn't. She was taken to a nursing home.

moments in her life. Often she frowns and shakes her head. "I just can't remember." But she has flashes — vignettes from the past — of riding the wagon down the hill into Weston for the first time, more than seventy years ago; the long cold walk to the outhouse in the winter; the pleasure of the summer kitchen, and above all the beauty of her mountains. They are like a few remaining pieces of a lost jig saw puzzle.

Betty Waite was six years old when her family took the train from Connecticut to Chester, Vermont, and then rode a horse and buggy to Weston where her father had found work in the general store. Betty went to the little schoolhouse in Weston and became best friends with Dottie Foster, Charley's sister. "We called each other 'sister-in-love,'" says Dottie. "I

remember Betty loved to read." She recalls the days she spent on the farm with Betty.

During World War II Dottie was writing her brother Charley, who was stationed in the South Pacific, and asked Betty if she would like to include a note. Charley and Betty began corresponding, and when Charley returned home the romance quickened. In 1947 he and Betty were married and moved to the family farm.

In the first years of their marriage Betty and Charley lived downstairs, his parents occupied the upstairs. There were hired hands to feed, and then came her five children. It was a time of endless cooking, washing, cleaning, gardening, and putting up preserves. Betty was known for her coffee cakes, but her happiest moments were picking raspberries and

Karen Lindbo — *Goat Farmer* — OAK KNOLL DAIRY FARM

Allison Hooper — *Cheese Maker* — VERMONT BUTTER AND CHEESE

This woman — Karen Lindbo — is charismatic. Her beauty is Nordic DNA: blond hair, hypnotic blue eyes, high cheekbones angling into a chin neither aggressive nor shallow, molding a classic profile put slightly off kilter by a bump in her nose. She is lean and supple, assertive but not aggressive. She presents her thoughts lucidly. Her body language says she likes men but her smile says her goats come first . . .

They don't have much for ears!

The Oak Knoll Dairy Farm, along the Connecticut River south of Windsor, Vermont, is the largest LaMancha goat farm (300, 175 milkers) in the country. LaMancha goats arrived with the first Spanish missionaries to California. Once nicknamed "monkeys," the bucks have gopher ears that are less than 1 inch in length and have no cartilage (the females have some cartilage in ears that can be up to 2 inches in length). In 1958 the LaMancha was officially recognized as an American breed, the first in the 8,500-year history of the domesticated goat.

Karen and her husband, George Redich, are baby boomers, and until 1989 they acted that way. Karen was brought up near Boston and helped, when she was young, on her grandfather's small cow and chicken farm. The farm was lost to suburbanization — taxes went up 200 percent in one year. "I was in junior high and decided I would never be interested in doing farming again," says Karen, seated in the spacious, neat, and cool dining room of their farmhouse. The house is very quiet, soothing.

She went on to become an architectural

designer, and her career soared as she worked for companies in Boston and Cambridge and traveled overseas to service foreign accounts. She then opened her own design firm and met her husband, a software developer (who, when he was young, helped out his grandfather on a blueberry farm; he was also in 4-H and raised fancy chickens and a beef cow).

The stepping-stone to goats came when they bought a horse stable in Winchester, Massachusetts, and Karen's brother gave her four LaMancha sheep for her birthday. Soon, however, they found there was not enough local hay for their horses or goats, so they scouted from Maine to Vermont for a hay farm to purchase. They finally bought the Windsor farm because Connecticut River Valley land is some of the richest in America, and it was only a couple hours' drive from their stable (and, according to Karen, she loved the old barn with the brick silo).

Soon she and her husband were showing their goats at fairs across the country. When they moved to Vermont, in 1989, after selling their other properties, they arrived with forty-five goats.

"I hated every single minute of the first year I was here," says Karen. "I was commuting back and forth to Boston, as I still had my design business, and I was milking goats and George had pulled out his back. That December the temperature did not rise above zero, and our house was poorly heated."

Still, it was good timing. The economy was taking a downward spiral, and Karen closed her design business. George had already quit his job, and they set up their responsibilities:

George would oversee the planting and harvest of corn, soybean, hay, and alfalfa on 138 acres of land, repair the machinery, and handle finances. Karen would be the herd manager.

"I never wanted to be an old designer anyway," said Karen. "It is a profession for young people and I was in it for fifteen years. Once you have a college

education, it doesn't matter what you do because you know how to process information."

Karen redesigned the barn stalls and arranged efficient methods of feeding. She designed a very compact milking parlor and bottling plant, so the flow of work moved quickly from the milking parlor to the pasteurizer, cooler, and bottling machine.

"Goat farming is the most challenging of all my jobs. It takes seven days, all hours, and you are totally responsible for the care of these animals; goats are very susceptible to disease; I am dealing with life and death, and this is enticing as I am in control. But farming is also a gamble, you are so dependent upon markets, weather, health." Karen reflects for a moment and then adds, "Our goats are

more than money producers, they are incredibly unique animals. I just really love these goats."

Karen has been off the farm once in four years, when her father died, and that was only for a day. She walks the property and works half a day with her sheepdog, whom she trains with a few Katahdin sheep that she keeps as pets. They now have two hired hands.

Oak Knoll produces every week 700 gallons of goat milk, which is distributed throughout the Northeast. Goat milk is naturally homogenized and has a smaller fat molecule than cow milk so that it is digested in twenty minutes rather than two hours. Oak Knoll milk is very clean and light. They also send 1,000 pounds of milk a month to Vermont Butter and Cheese, which turns their milk into goat cheese.

"When we started our farm we didn't realize that Vermont Butter and Cheese, which is an hour away, processes goat cheese. About a year after we set up our farm we called Allison Hooper at the company and she said no, she didn't need anymore milk. Six months later she called back and asked how soon could we ship milk. That was really the beginning of our commercial goat dairy."

Allison Hooper is also an attractive woman, but she is not in love with goats so much as making cheese and butter. She has red hair, most often hidden by the hair net workers are required to wear in their Barre, Vermont, plant. She has a friendly relationship with her employees and an organized mind behind her smile. Her goal is to produce cheese and butter as good as the French make in Normandy and the Haute Alpes, where she first learned their methods of making cheese and butter.

"I was a French major in college in Connecticut and spent two semesters in Paris. I needed a summer job and went to Brittany and worked as an intern on a farm that had forty goats and thirteen cows. They made charcuterie, fresh and aged goat cheese, crème fraiche, fromage blanc, farm butter, and cow's milk cheese. That was in 1980. After graduating from college, I returned to France and worked in the Alps, where they made a little round goat cheese and processed honey. I loved the lifestyle and the craft of operating small farms. They sold their cheese on the Riviera to stores and restaurants, and I thought it would be a dream to do this in the United States."

When she returned, Allison worked in her home state of New Jersey for a woman who had a goat herd, but, wanting to be her own boss, in 1983 she moved to Vermont; she had the idea that Vermont was a cheese maker's sort of place. Allison milked goats on a small farm in Brookfield and worked in the testing lab for the Agriculture Department. She didn't make any cheese until she was invited to a chefs' dinner in Stowe. Anton Flory, the chef in charge, wanted some goat cheese, so she made a batch on her kitchen stove. The chefs loved it and left her their business cards. She was seated with Bob Reece — who worked in the Agriculture Development division — and his wife, Sandy, who suggested that Allison and Bob get together and form a business. Alison had the expertise in making cheese; Bob had an MBA in finance and was at the time involved in the development of the specialty food market.

In the fall of 1984 they quit their jobs and incorporated Vermont Butter and Cheese. With small loans they bought a boiler, a cooler, and a pickup and began picking up milk from goat farms and bot-

tling it and making cheese. They had a distributor in Boston who, shortly after they were in operation, said he didn't need more milk. That forced them into making only cheese. Allison worked seven days a week making cheese, and Bob delivered it to Vermont stores in the pickup. By 1987 they moved into an industrial park in Barre and set up a plant to produce cheese and also butter.

"We learned," says Allison, "that to survive we couldn't just run around and sell goat cheese to Vermont stores. Vermonters do not pay high prices for quality food, so we found a distributor in Boston and were all of a sudden getting big orders for the Boston stores. Then in 1987 we attended the Fancy Food Show in New York City. We were the darling of the show for the French franc doubled in value and all of a sudden French goat

cheese was twice as expensive, and our product was very good."

The timing was right in the culinary world. Goat cheese was becoming a favorite with many chefs at tony restaurants. It was also at the time the two partners refinanced their business. They closed these arrangements in 1987, just before the stock crash.

In their new plant they began making all the products Allison first made in France — several types of goat cheese, fromage blanc, crème fraiche, and cultured butter.

"I have to say at first we made awful cheese," recounts Allison. "But now we are making a very quality product. We have to, to compete against the French."

Today, the franc is low, and the subsidies French small farms receive from their government is higher,

so their cheese and butter can be sold in the United States at fairly low prices. Allison knows that her products have to be equal to the French. To that end in, 2002, she and Bob have hired France's leading goat cheese expert to help redesign their plant.

"We have to streamline our product line to make it more compatible. We can't age a little ripened goat cheese with a big wheel; there are different bacteria and molds that are not compatible in the same building. You need different aging rooms. It is a huge expense to set up correctly."

Allison's passion to make a perfect cheese has helped the Vermont cheese industry grow. She was one of the first in Vermont to make cheese to be sold in stores. There are now thirty cheese makers who belong to the Vermont Cheese Council, a group Allison started. In addition, Vermont Butter and Cheese picks up milk from twenty-three goat farms, fourteen of which are in Vermont. She also buys milk and cream from the St. Albans Cooperative and Booth Brothers for their cultured butter and soft cream cheeses.

In 2001 Vermont Butter and Cheese did $4.1 million in business, selling their goat cheeses, cream cheeses, and butter throughout the East Coast of the United States. They have twenty-two employees.

"I think many goat farms are in existence here in Vermont because we are the only buyer in the region. We provided a much broader market for them. Our smallest farm has about thirty goats, the largest three hundred. What they want to do is farm and have the milk disappear. We do that for them."

Kelly von Trapp — *Dairy Farmer* — von Trapp Farm

The Common Road, most of it dirt, runs along a plateau above the town of Waitsfield. Across the valley to the west is the backbone of the Green Mountains; etched on its flanks are the ski resorts of Mad River Glen and Sugarbush. It is a glorious view, and desirous. Half a century ago only farms and hay fields stretched along the plateau, now many of the cow barns have been renovated into stables for horses. White fences so loved by the horse people demarcate the pastures filled not with Jerseys or Holsteins but Morgans, Thoroughbreds, and polo ponies. Trophy houses, a couple of developments, and numerous smaller homes have been built along the plateau. Some owners visit only in the summer, others are skiers, and all wish to retire here unless they have a home in Palm Beach.

Not far from Waitsfield Common, on the east side of the road, partially hidden by huge maples, is a brick house that was built in 1810. The barn facing the house was constructed a century later. Farm machinery sits comfortably in the yard. In front of one of the maples is a sign that says Maple Syrup For Sale. Martin and Kelly von Trapp live in the brick farmhouse. Martin is a son of one of the singing von Trapps of *Sound of Music* fame. His wife, Kelly, is a Blauvelt, who was brought up in Waterbury. Martin's parents bought the farm in 1959. In 1979, Martin and Kelly, who were just married, took it over.

"I didn't know what I was getting into," says Kelly, a small, attractive woman with a sculpted face and a happy smile; she looks much younger than forty-three. "But I'm an outdoors person, and I like doing physical work. I didn't know how much I care for animals, and it all sort of grew on me. I guess this has been what I was meant to do."

"What I found is so important for me is working alongside my husband and sometimes with the children. I do spend many hours working alone, but there is always that feeling of teamwork and being together that is important."

In the morning Kelly milks the forty head of Jerseys; Martin milks in the evening. She does barn

chores and then tends to the house. He does the fieldwork. She is the book keeper and maintains a large garden. He repairs the machinery. He cuts wood; she splits it. They share sugaring chores. During haying season Martin mows, she rakes and is the stacker. They also raised three children, the youngest of which is eighteen.

This is a happy farm, you can feel it with the cows, calves, and sheep who are not afraid to be touched and the closeness between Kelly and Martin when they are working or talking with friends.

"I feel it is a simple hardworking life," said Kelly, and that is particularly true in haying season. They mow their and neighbors' fields, and they make square bales. Kelly does the raking and stacks the bales in the hay wagon that is then driven into the

upper section of the barn, where it is unloaded and again stacked. When it is needed bales are dumped through trap doors to the milking stalls.

"It is hot, dusty work, but I like it," said Kelly. She will pick up and stack as many as 900 bales a day, 10,000 in a season. This hands-on method is, as the experts would say, labor intensive, but it works best with the von Trapp's old barn and equipment. They feel no reason to invest in new and expensive round-bale machinery. "Besides," said Kelly, "I don't like all that white plastic."

In the past Kelly and Martin always had their children to help out with the haying, but now they are grown and away.

"I don't know if any of them will have an interest in running this farm, but then again, we have a number of years left in us . . . we'll see. They have learned many skills on this farm, and responsibilities . . . perhaps we'll find someone young who would come here for room and board and lend a hand . . . a hired hand can be financially difficult."

The traffic on the Common Road in front of their house is a barometer to the change in Waitsfield. It is not cars so much as bicyclists, joggers, people walking their dogs, horseback riders.

"One drawback in being a dairy farmer is the commitment to twice a day, 365 days a year having to tend to the animals. It is hard to ever go anywhere for more than a few hours. This is something that people with weekends free or weeks off might not realize.

"I feel good at farming and have satisfaction in preserving our landscape. I can find peace in a cow pasture, field, or woods, but sometimes I wonder if it is appreciated. All our neighbors and our community like having farms and open lands. We pay $6,000 a year in taxes, and some will say, with our 100 acres, that is not much, but it is a big chunk taken out of our income. I feel we are doing a service to the community and to the state. The towns don't give much to farmers, although we make it more attractive to tourists."

They have thought of selling the rights to the land trust but were told by the land trust people that they wanted to also conserve adjoining property before they would invest but would be most happy if the von Trapps donated the development rights to them. "We're not wealthy enough to do that," said Kelly.

Kelly and Martin von Trapp and the other farm people in this book are demonstrating that it is possible for a family or a couple to create a life with a sense of fulfillment to themselves and their community, and to do it with just a small patch of land.

Directory — Listed below are the farm women featured in this book, their addresses, and the products they produce and sell.

Bartholomew, Clare and Jeanne *(page 52)*
Bartholomew Brothers Farm
3934 East Road, Benson, VT 05743. Tel. 802.537.3934
Tel. for Clare: 802.537.4932
Bulk milk shipped to Garelick; maple syrup, hay, lumber,
   logs, gravel
Jeanne Bartholomew also sells real estate.

Bailey, Janet *(page 50)*
Fair Winds Farm
511 Upper Dummerston Road Brattleboro, VT 05301
E-mail: fairwind@sover.net; Website: sover.net/~fwjzbail
Perennial plants, draft horse workshops, Suffolk Punch horses,
   piglets, eggs, sleigh rides
Sells at Brattleboro Farmers' Market.

Burke, Anne and Becky *(page 40)*
Harvest Hill Farm
83 Stewart Road, Berlin, VT 05602. Tel. 802.223.7927
Bulk milk shipped to Agri-Mark; maple syrup, registered
   Ayrshires, Norwegian elkhounds, Christmas wreaths and gar-
   lands; water dowsing

Carpenter, Barbara *(page 62)*
Carpenter Farm
PO Box 93, Cabot, VT 05647 Tel. 802.426.3331
Organic bulk milk to Horizon, Inc; maple syrup, forest products

Chalmers, Carrie *(page 44)*
Quoyburray Farm
7 Greendale Road, Weston, VT 05161. Tel. 802.824.6400.
E-mail: cchalmers@mailcity.com
Annuals, perennials, vegetable and herb plants, vegetables
Sells at farmers' market in Londonderry.

Day, Ann *(page 28)*
Knoll Farm/Back Four House
PO Box 300, 732 Bragg Hill Road, Fayston, VT 05673.
   Tel. 802.496.3527
Scottish Highland cattle

Dunsmore, Carol *(page 36)*
Fayre Farm
1974 Dunsmore Road, Swanton, VT 05488. Tel. 802.524.4819
Freezer lambs, replacement dairy heifers, Leicester ewe lambs,
   Morgan horses

Dwyer, Pam *(page 102)*
Wild Branch Tree Farm
53 Heath Road, Wolcott, VT 05680. Tel. 802.888.2783

E-mail pdwyer@pshift.com
Christmas trees, wholesale and retail; wreaths and greens

Eastman, Barbara *(page 18)*
Eastman Farm
435 Town House Road, Addison, VT 05491. Tel. 802.759.2764
Bulk milk shipped to St. Albans Cooperative

Ellis-Thurber, Amanda *(page 112)*
Lilac Ridge Farm
264 Ames Hill Road, Brattleboro, VT 05303.
   Tel. 802.257.0985/802.254.8113
Bulk milk shipped to Agri-Mark; maple syrup, organically grown
   vegetables, cut flowers, Christmas trees, hardwood and soft-
   wood logs
Sells at Brattleboro Farmers' Market.

Fischer, Mary Beth *(page 90)*
Fischer Farm
143 Lawrence Road
Springfield, VT 05156. Tel. 802.463.3018
Feeder pigs, roasters, freezer hogs (whole or half), freezer beef
   (one-quarter or larger), live beef calves; custom order cuts
Delivery within 40–50 miles.

Fondiller, Laini *(page 21)*
Lazy Lady Farm
934 Snyder Brook Road, Westfield, VT 05874. Tel. 802744.6365
E-mail: laini@sover.net
One dozen types of goat cheese, cheese-making classes
Distributed by Provisions International, White River Junction,
   VT, and sells at Montpelier Farmers' Market.

Freeman, Bambi *(page 72)*
Sterling Brook Farm
Sterling Valley Road, Stowe, VT 05672. Tel. 802.888.3735
Lamb meat, wool yarn, wool blankets, hats, sheepskins, pastured
   chickens, eggs, composted manure
Sells at home and ships mail order. Sells at Waitsfield, Waterbury,
   and Stowe farmers' markets.
"I would not be able to farm by myself without my Border collies,
   Roy and Gaelen, and my old-world guard dog, Yugo."

Goodall, Pat *(page 76)*
Borderline Ratites Farm
1052 Goodall Road, Derby Line, VT 05839. Tel. 802.895.4541
E-mail: goodall@together.net
Emu oil and emollients, retail and wholesale
Ship mail order. Brochure available.

Goodrich, Sally *(page 69)*
Molly Brook Farms
76 Cow Hill Road, West Danville, VT 05873. Tel. 802.563.2579
E-mail: mbrook@together.net. Website:
   www.mollybrook.usjersey.com
Bulk milk shipped to Agri-Mark; registered Jersey cattle and
   embryos.
Sells at the farm and wholesale.

Goodridge, Colleen *(page 48)*
Goodridge Lumber, Inc.
PO 515, Albany, VT 05820. Tel. 802.755.6298. Fax. 802.755.6160
White cedar logs for log homes, decking, interior, log siding
"White cedar is rot resistant, light, and good insulation. Come up
   and we'll show you one of our log homes."

Hamilton, Ellen H. *(page 120)*
Sunny Hill Farm
414 Hamilton Road, Brattleboro, VT 05301. Tel. 802.254.2664
Ship bulk milk to Agri-Mark; maple syrup and wood products
"My son Kevin and his wife Jean run the farm. Tel. 802.257.5666."

Hazelton, Debbie *(page 60)*
Hell's Creek Farm, Holden Road, Londonderry, VT. 05148
Tel. 802.824.6881
Homeopathy, forest management

Hodges, Kate *(page 57)*
Sunrise Orchards
1287 N. Bingham Street, Cornwall, VT 05753. Tel. 802.777.8038
Apples distributed by ourselves and others; artwork for sale
"Sunrise Orchards is a fully approved CORE Values Northeast
   farm. It uses Integrated Pest Management (IPM) production
   methods to control pests. Write for further information.
   Viewing of sculpture installations and 'tree art.' Commissioned
   art work is available upon request."

Hooper, Allison *(page 126)*
Vermont Butter and Cheese Company
PO Box 95, Websterville, VT 05678. Tel. 802.479.9371
Fresh and aged goat cheeses, cultured butter, mascarpone, crème
   fraiche, fromage blanc, quark
Distributed nationally through specialty and natural food
   retailers.
"We ship mail order only if the customer cannot find our cheese
   in their local market."

Jarvis, Sylvia   *(page 92)*
Jarvis Farm
201 Jarvis Road
East Braintree, VT 05060. Tel. 802.728.5373
Fresh-cut hay

Johnson, Debbie and Laurie   *(page 24)*
Saga-Morgans
314 Murphy Hill Road, North Bennington, VT 05257.
   Tel. 802.442.5945
E-mail: sagamrgn@together.net
Registered Morgan horses, grass-fed beef in season.
Sell at home and wholesale.
"Pen & ink artwork with a rural flavor."

Kaiman, Lisa   *(page 32)*
Jersey Girls Dairy
157 Thomspon Road
Chester, VT 05143. Tel. 802.875.6576
E-mail: jgirls@vermontel.net
Ships bulk milk to Agri-Mark
"We strive for cow comfort toward health and profitability!"

Landauer, Debbie, and Rebecca Moyer   *(page 16)*
Northern Prize Garlic
For information about garlic, call 802.933.2820.

Lazor, Anne   *(page 96)*
Butterworks Farm
421 Trumpass Road, Westfield, VT 05874. Tel. 802.744.6855
Website in progress: www.butterworksfarm.com
Yogurt, heavy cream, cheddar cheese
Distributed through Northeast Co-ops, United Natural Foods,
   Dayville, CT, covering the Northeast, south to Georgia and
   west to Ohio.
"We have internships for inspired individuals."

Leroy, Karen Cadow   *(page 82)*
Popoma Farm
202 West Road, Whiting, VT 05778. Tel./Fax 802.623.6220
E-mail: popoma@juno.com; Website: www.popoma.com
Dried flowers and herb wreaths, potpourri, sachets, herbal reme-
   dies, wedding flowers, flavorings, livestock, and hay

Lindbo, Karen   *(page 126)*
Oak Knoll Dairy
Route 5, Windsor, VT 05089. Tel. 802.674.5426
E-mail: oakknoll@turbont.net
Ship bulk goat milk to Vermont Butter and Cheese, Websterville,
   VT; bottle and sell Grade A pasteurized goat milk — whole
   milk, 2% reduced fat, half and half, and chocolate (bottled in
   half gallons, quarts, and pints); 50-pound bags of shelled corn
   and hay
Sell at home and throughout the northeast and mid-Atlantic
   states through Northeast Distributors of Brattleboro.
"We only bottle and sell milk produced by our own goats."

Neff, Mimi   *(page 122)*
Little Holden Farm
96 Holden Hill, Weston, VT 05161. Tel. 802.824.6485
Holstein replacement heifers

Pollack, Marian; Susman, Marjorie   *(page 98)*
Orb Weaver Farm
3406 Lime Kiln Road, New Haven, VT 05472. Tel. 802.877.3755
E-mail: orbweavr@together.net
Orb Weaver Vermont Farmhouse cheese, cave aged cheese,
   organic vegetables
Mail order, write or e-mail for catalog.
"Please call before visiting. Our cheese is made from milk pro-
   duced by our own Jersey herd."

Pomeroy, Marian   *(page 108)*
Pomeroy Farm
1660 Middletown Road, Londonderry, VT 05148. Tel.
   802.824.5489
E-mail: pomeroy@sover.net
Bulk milk shipped to Agri-Mark; farmhouse cheese, eggs, lamb,
   beef, and veal
Sell at farmers' markets in Londonderry, Manchester, Rutland,
   and Boston at Government Square.
"We ship mail cheese mail order. Tours by appointment or luck."

Ratcliff, Lydia   *(page 78)*
Lovejoy Brook Farm
2604 East Hill Road, Andover, VT 05143. Tel. and Fax
   802.875.3159
Website: www.northeastgoatgenetics.com
Vermont Fancy Meats, a cooperative at this address, distributes
   fresh goat meat, veal, and other meat products from Vermont
   farmers to restaurants in New England and New York City.
   Northeast Dairy Associates, also at this address, sells goats and
   semen from New England to other countries. This Website is
   also in Portugese.

Ravenelle, Deb   *(page 116)*
Sterling Mountain Farm
1064 Upper French Hill Road, Johnson, VT 05656. Tel.
   802.635.1741
Maple syrup wholesale and retail and mail order, horse logging,
   horse carriage service
"Call or write and we will ship maple syrup to you."

Rooney, Charlene   *(page 66)*
Rooney Farm
2693 Mud City Loop, Morrisville, VT 05661. Tel. 802.888.2729
Bulk milk shipped to Horizon Organic Milk; maple syrup retail
   and mail order.

Rubaud, Julie   *(page 104)*
Eric and Julie's Plants and Produce
205 Cemetery Road, Starksboro, VT 05437
Salad greens, vegetables, winter squash, herb plants

Distribution from Burlington to Rutland through Deep Root
   Trucking Co-op, Squash Valley.
"We offer a subscription program where members of the community buy a share of the season's harvest and come each week to
   pick up their vegetables."

Seeley, Maggie   *(page 14)*
2886 Mountain Road, Weybridge, VT 05753. Tel. 802.545.2123
Nop Brothers and Sons Farm is in Salisbury, and ships milk to St
   Albans Coop.

Shumway, Ruth   *(page 114)*
Green Acres Milking Shorthorns
2925 VT Route 14 South Randolph, VT 05060. Tel. 802.728.4961
Bulk milk shipped to Agri-Mark; breeders of registered Milking
   Shorthorn cattle; sell calves for 4-H projects and selected older
   animals

Smith, Annette   *(page 84)*
Blue Beech Farm
789 Baker Brook Road, Danby, VT 05739. Tel. 802.446.2094
E-mail: pursebox@vermontel.net
Fresh eggs may be purchased at New Morning Natural Foods,
   Manchester, Vermont.

von Trapp, Kelly   *(page 130)*
von Trapp Farm
251 Common Road, Waitsfield, VT 05673
Ship bulk milk to Agri-Mark; maple syrup.

Wallace, Rosina   *(page 10)*
Wallace Farm
1903 Blush Hill Road, Waterbury, VT 05676. Tel. 802.244.6954
Ship bulk milk to Agri-Mark

Wolcott, Julie   *(page 104)*
Green Wind Farm
Fairfield, VT. Tel 802.933.4592
(mailing address. 1345 Northrop Road, Enosburg Falls, VT
   05450)
Bulk milk shipped to St. Albans Co-op Creamery. Sell at home
   raw milk, maple syrup, strawberries, and first-cut dry hay; mail
   order maple syrup.
Distributors for maple syrup: Butternut Farms, Tyler Place, Rail
   City Market. Sometimes sell at Fairfield Farmers' Market.
Farm mentor for Franklin, Grand Isle Counties through
   Northeast Organic Farm Association, which connects farms to
   school programs and food service providers.
"I can't underestimate the value of a supportive household, my
   partner, and our growing children who find value and purpose
   in this unusual — for this day and age — lifestyle. To all of us,
   it makes sense, most of the time, as the American culture swirls
   out of control. Amen."